Ka-BOOM! Create Your Own Manga Adventures

A BLANK COMIC BOOK FOR KIDS

YANCEY LABAT

ROCKRIDGE PRESS

Copyright © 2020 by Rockridge Press, Emeryville, California

No part of this publication may be reproduced, stored in a retrieval system, or transmitted in any form or by any means, electronic, mechanical, photocopying, recording, scanning, or otherwise, except as permitted under Sections 107 or 108 of the 1976 United States Copyright Act, without the prior written permission of the Publisher. Requests to the Publisher for permission should be addressed to the Permissions Department, Rockridge Press, 6005 Shellmound Street, Suite 175, Emeryville, CA 94608.

Limit of Liability/Disclaimer of Warranty: The Publisher and the author make no representations or warranties with respect to the accuracy or completeness of the contents of this work and specifically disclaim all warranties, including without limitation warranties of fitness for a particular purpose. No warranty may be created or extended by sales or promotional materials. The advice and strategies contained herein may not be suitable for every situation. This work is sold with the understanding that the Publisher is not engaged in rendering medical, legal, or other professional advice or services. If professional assistance is required, the services of a competent professional person should be sought. Neither the Publisher nor the author shall be liable for damages arising herefrom. The fact that an individual, organization, or website is referred to in this work as a citation and/or potential source of further information does not mean that the author or the Publisher endorses the information the individual, organization, or website may provide or recommendations they/it may make. Further, readers should be aware that websites listed in this work may have changed or disappeared between when this work was written and when it is read.

For general information on our other products and services or to obtain technical support, please contact our Customer Care Department within the United States at (866) 744-2665, or outside the United States at (510) 253-0500.

Rockridge Press publishes its books in a variety of electronic and print formats. Some content that appears in print may not be available in electronic books, and vice versa.

TRADEMARKS: Rockridge Press and the Rockridge Press logo are trademarks or registered trademarks of Callisto Media Inc. and/or its affiliates, in the United States and other countries, and may not be used without written permission. All other trademarks are the property of their respective owners. Rockridge Press is not associated with any product or vendor mentioned in this book.

Interior and Cover Designer: Julie Schrader
Art Producer: Janice Ackerman
Editor: Cathy Hennessy
Illustrations: © 2020 Yancey Labat.

ISBN: Print 978-1-64611-809-0
R0

To Eliza and Serenna

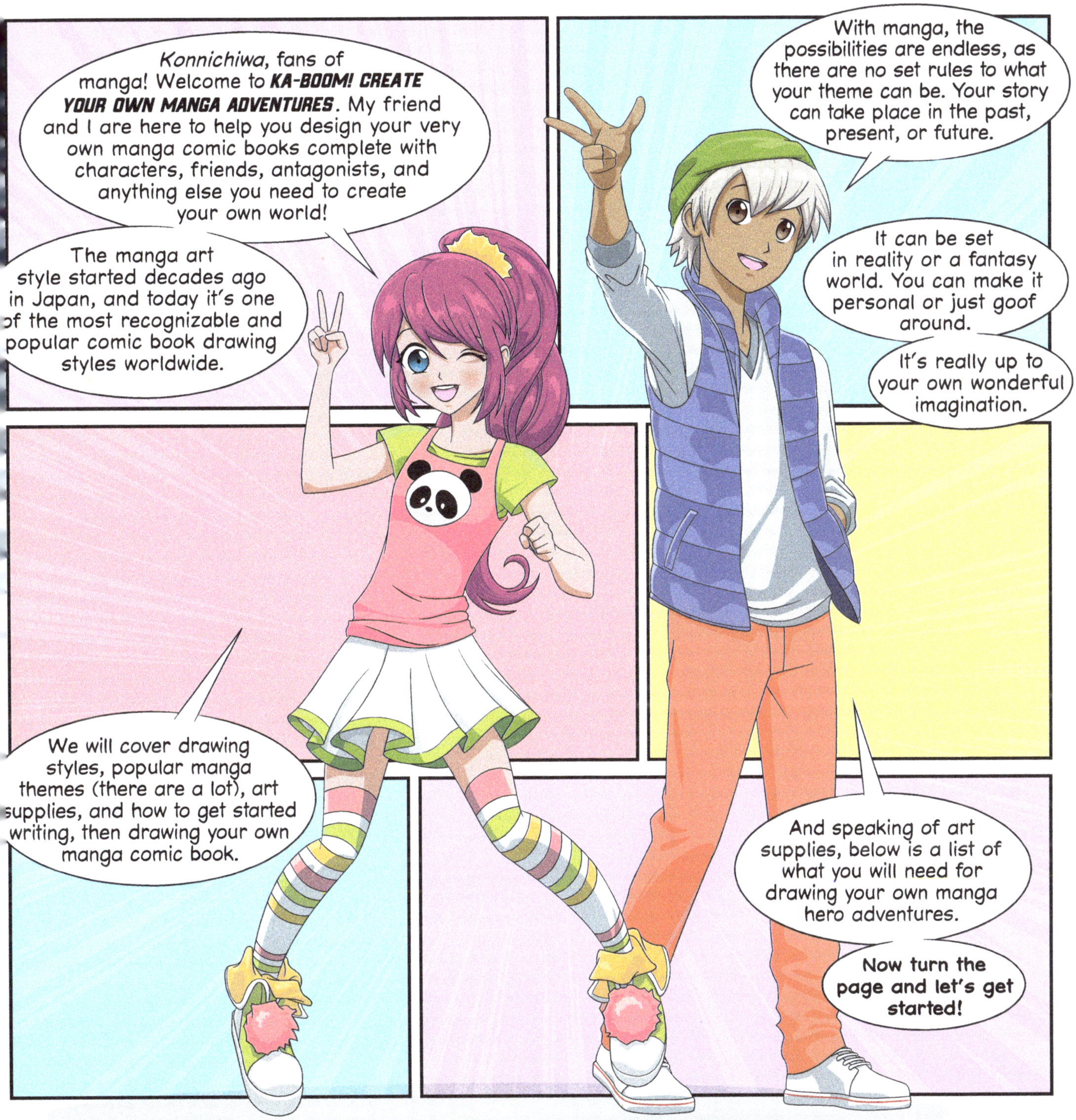
Konnichiwa, fans of manga! Welcome to ***KA-BOOM! CREATE YOUR OWN MANGA ADVENTURES***. My friend and I are here to help you design your very own manga comic books complete with characters, friends, antagonists, and anything else you need to create your own world!
The manga art style started decades ago in Japan, and today it's one of the most recognizable and popular comic book drawing styles worldwide.
With manga, the possibilities are endless, as there are no set rules to what your theme can be. Your story can take place in the past, present, or future.
It can be set in reality or a fantasy world. You can make it personal or just goof around.
It's really up to your own wonderful imagination.
We will cover drawing styles, popular manga themes (there are a lot), art supplies, and how to get started writing, then drawing your own manga comic book.
And speaking of art supplies, below is a list of what you will need for drawing your own manga hero adventures.
Now turn the page and let's get started!

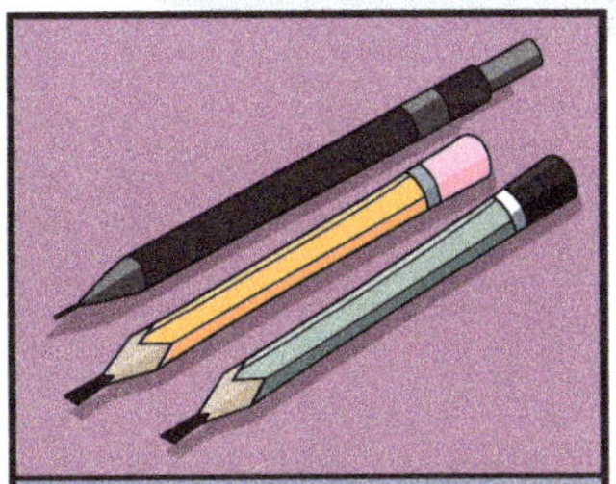

Pencils

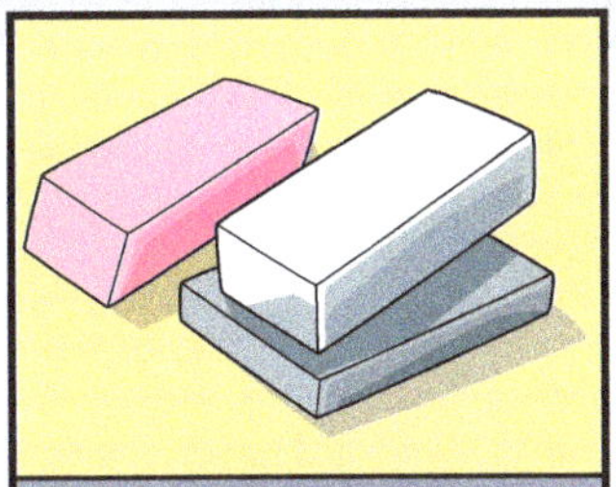

Erasers

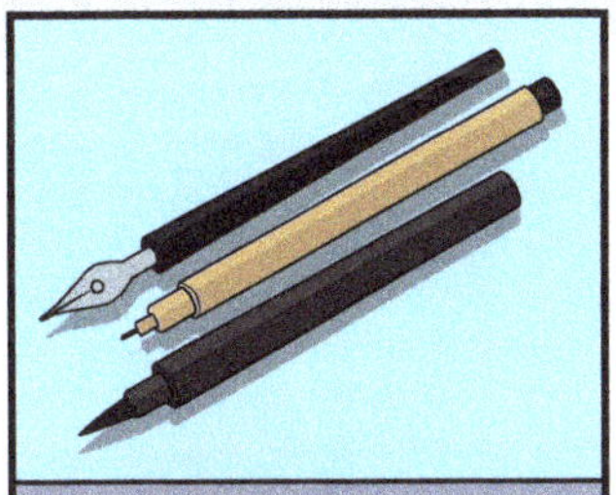

Pens for inking

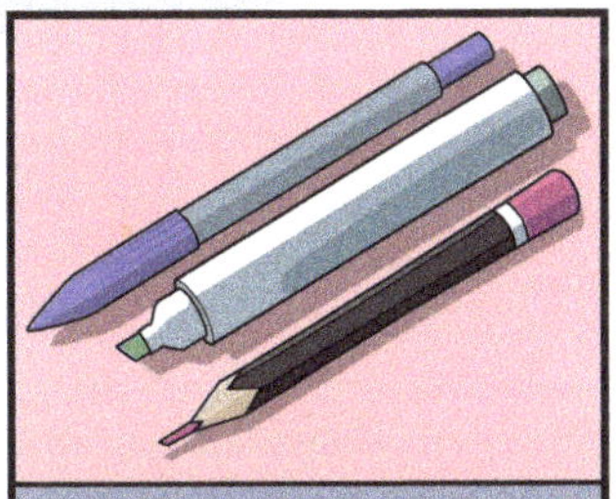

Colored Pencils/Markers*

*Markers may bleed through the page, so test before using.

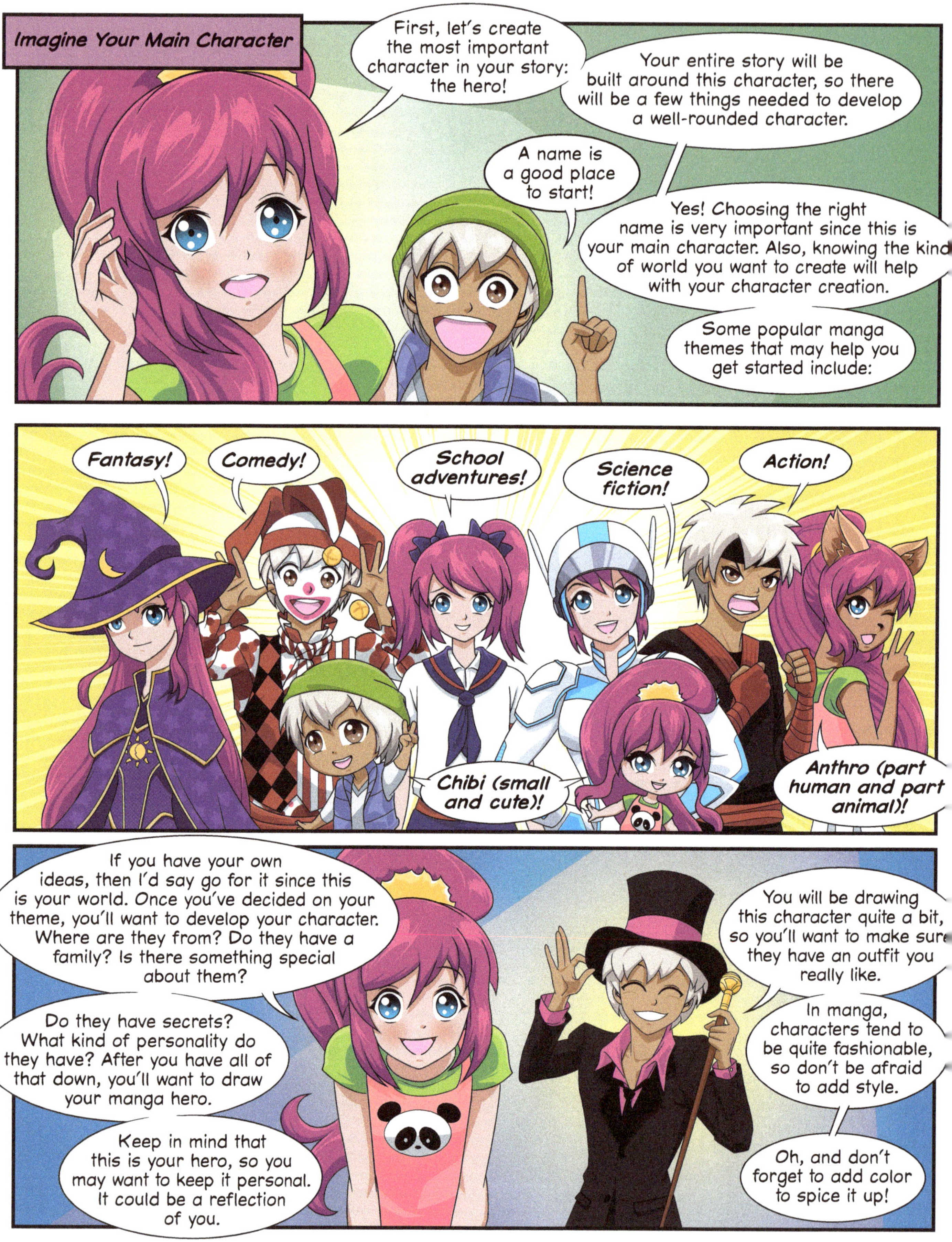
Imagine Your Main Character
First, let's create the most important character in your story: the hero!
Your entire story will be built around this character, so there will be a few things needed to develop a well-rounded character.
A name is a good place to start!
Yes! Choosing the right name is very important since this is your main character. Also, knowing the kind of world you want to create will help with your character creation.
Some popular manga themes that may help you get started include:
Fantasy!
Comedy!
School adventures!
Science fiction!
Action!
Chibi (small and cute)!
Anthro (part human and part animal)!
If you have your own ideas, then I'd say go for it since this is your world. Once you've decided on your theme, you'll want to develop your character. Where are they from? Do they have a family? Is there something special about them?
Do they have secrets? What kind of personality do they have? After you have all of that down, you'll want to draw your manga hero.
Keep in mind that this is your hero, so you may want to keep it personal. It could be a reflection of you.
You will be drawing this character quite a bit, so you'll want to make sur they have an outfit you really like.
In manga, characters tend to be quite fashionable, so don't be afraid to add style.
Oh, and don't forget to add color to spice it up!

Manga Drawing Style

There are many variations to manga facial features, but most are based on the same idea of large, round eyes; small, simple mouths; and a single slightly bent line for a nose. This is just a general guide to drawing the facial features. Yours may vary, and that's perfectly fine. Remember, the idea is to have fun!

The Head

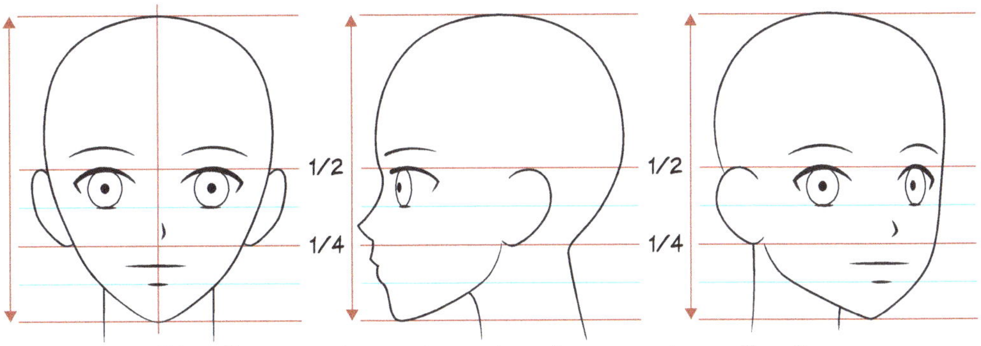

1/2
1/4
1/2
1/4

The diagram above shows how to properly section the head for placing facial features.

Eyes

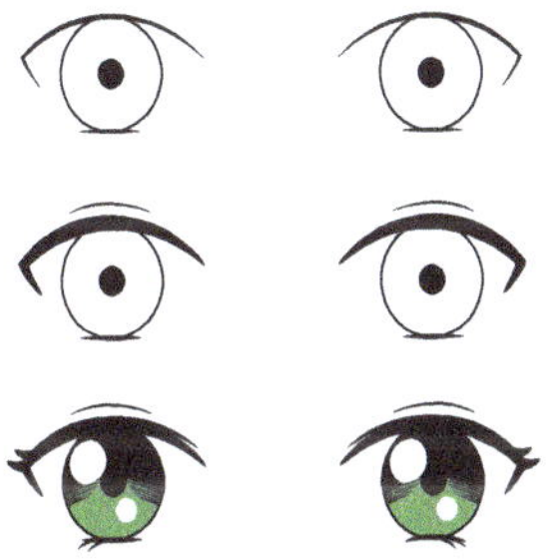

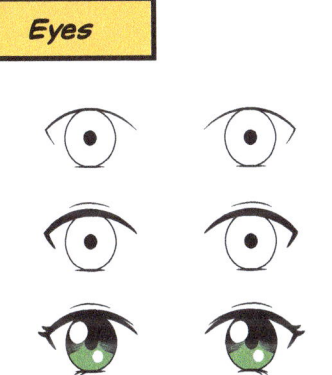

The upper eyelids are drawn in an arc, while the lower are smaller and flatter. The pupil is a small dot in the center of the eye. Then add shading.

Mouth and Nose

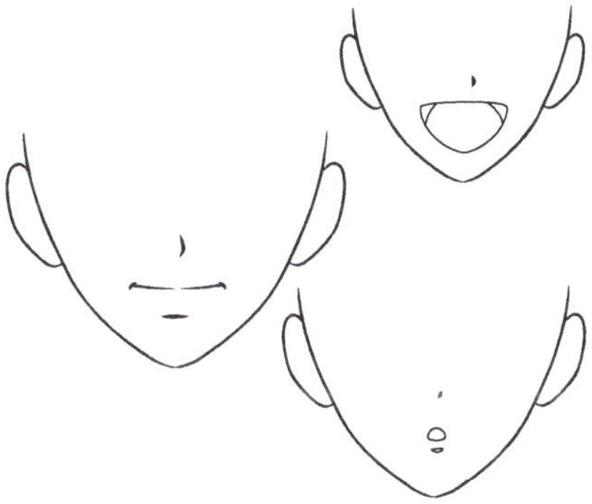

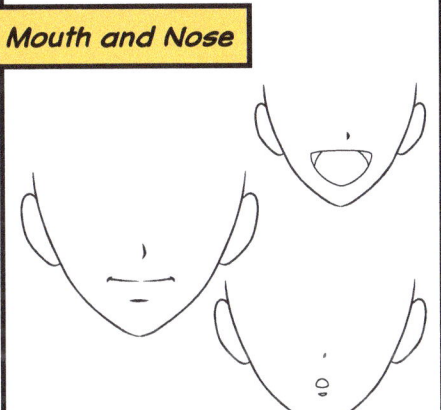

Mouths are very simple and rarely have full lips. The nose is even more simplistic, usually in the shape of a bent line or even a dot.

Facial Expressions

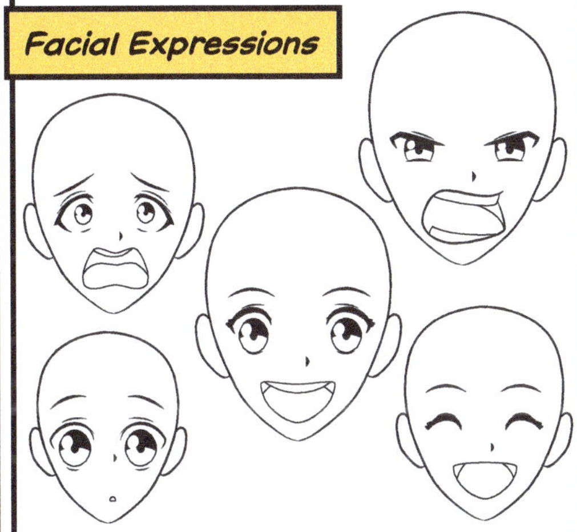

Facial expressions can be greatly exaggerated based on the character's mood. Have fun with these!

Hair

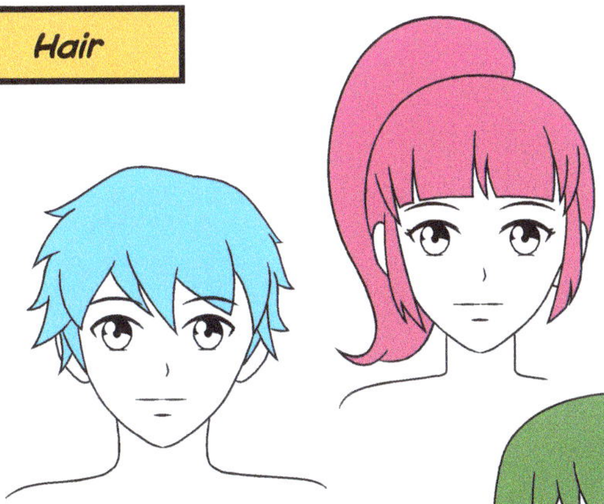

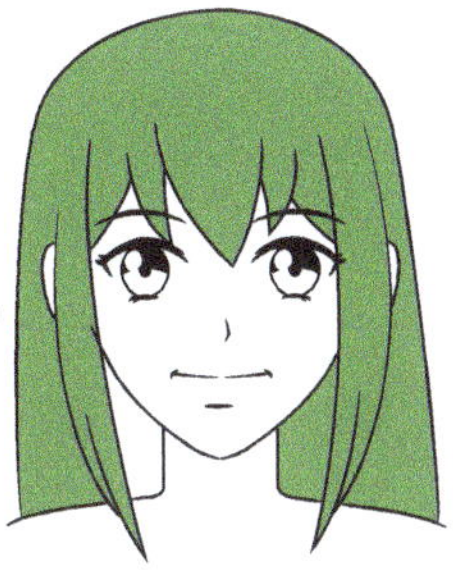

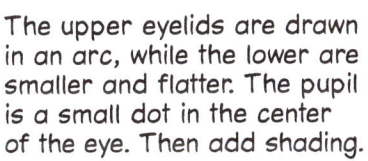

Manga hair is drawn in clumps and shapes rather than strands. It tends to be spiky or messy in boys. Bangs are popular for girls' hair, and colorful hair is quite common for any gender.

Clothing

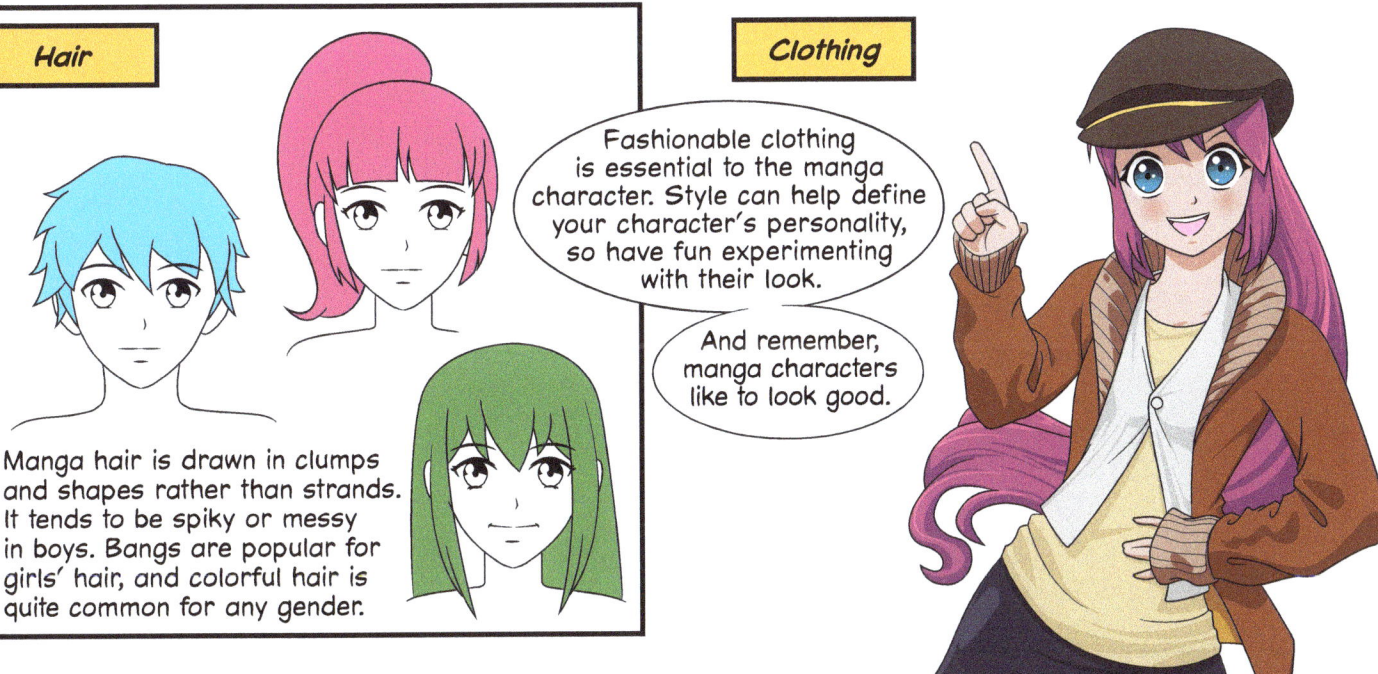

Fashionable clothing is essential to the manga character. Style can help define your character's personality, so have fun experimenting with their look.

And remember, manga characters like to look good.

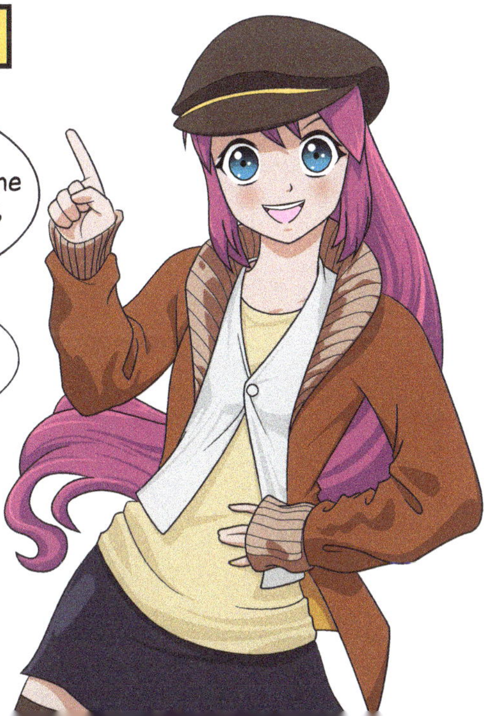

Sketch Your Main Character Here!

Imagine and Sketch Your Main Character's Sidekick and Other Characters

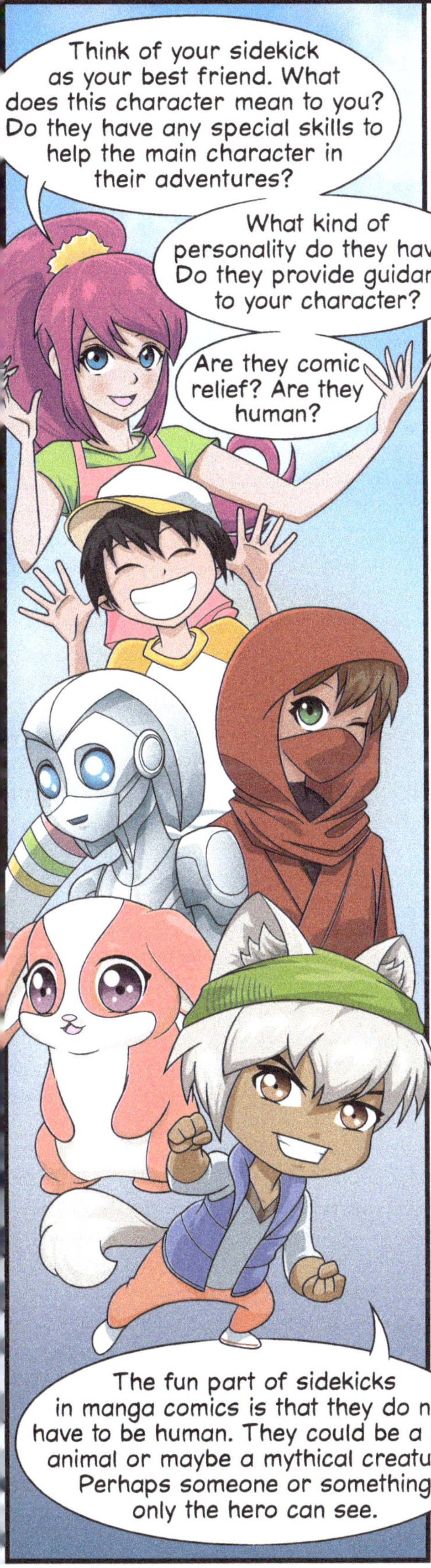
Think of your sidekick as your best friend. What does this character mean to you? Do they have any special skills to help the main character in their adventures?
What kind of personality do they have? Do they provide guidance to your character?
Are they comic relief? Are they human?
The fun part of sidekicks in manga comics is that they do not have to be human. They could be a cute animal or maybe a mythical creature. Perhaps someone or something only the hero can see.

Sketch your sidekick here!

Imagine and Sketch Your Main Character's World

This is your world, so have fun creating it! It can be anywhere your imagination wants it to be—Earth, space, a magical land, another planet, a different time period like the past or the future. Your entire story may take place here, so plan it well. A few questions you may want to ask yourself when planning are . . .

What is the name of the place your manga character lives?

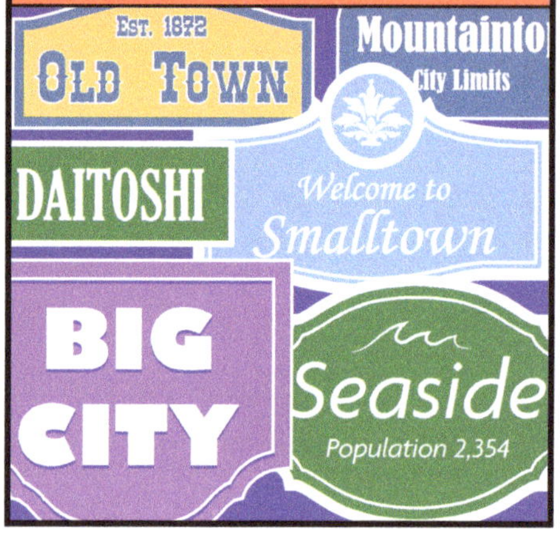

EST. 1872
OLD TOWN
Mountainto
City Limits
DAITOSHI
Welcome to Smalltown
BIG CITY
Seaside
Population 2,354

Where do they live? A city? The country? Outer space?

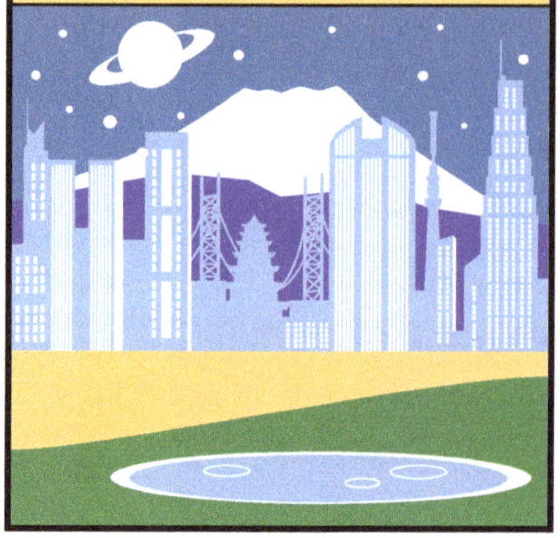

Sketch your world here!

What does their home look like?

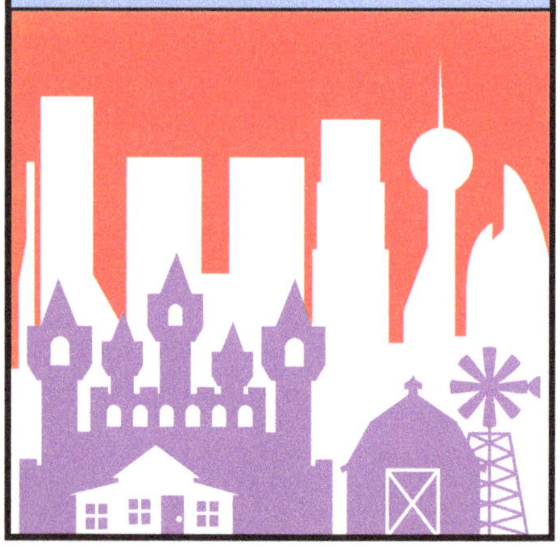

Do they live alone or with others? Do they have pets?

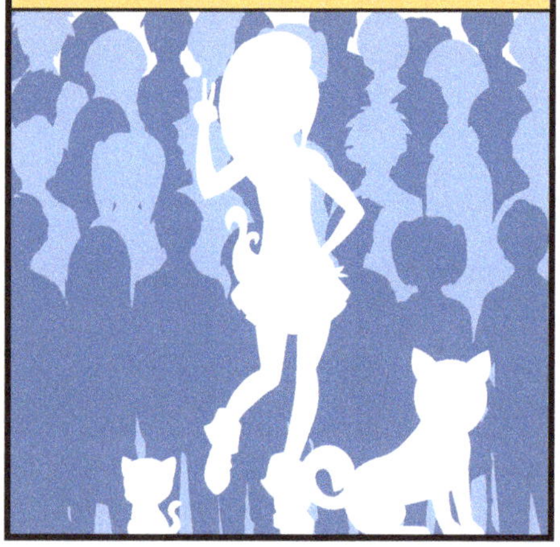

Are there any threats or conflicts in this world?

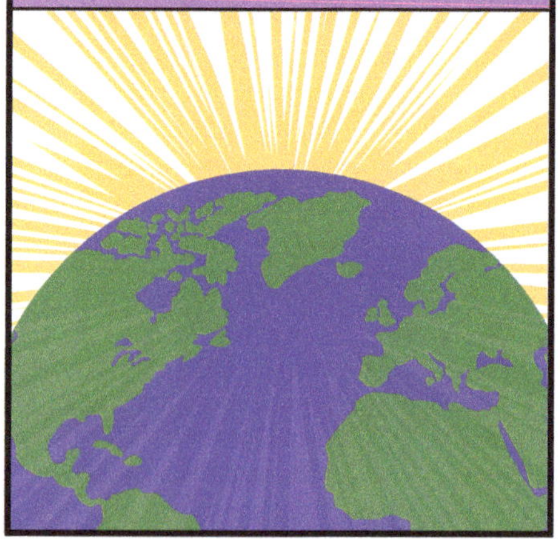

Imagine and Sketch Your Main Character's Vehicles, Gadgets, and Accessories

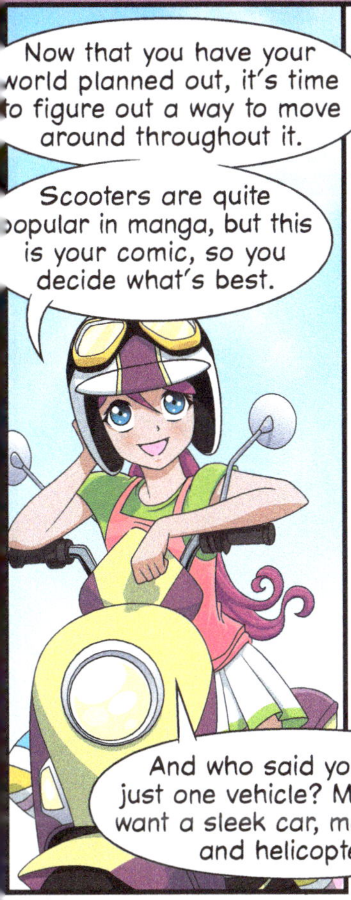
Now that you have your world planned out, it's time to figure out a way to move around throughout it.
Scooters are quite popular in manga, but this is your comic, so you decide what's best.
And who said you need just one vehicle? Maybe you want a sleek car, motorcycle, and helicopter!

Sketch your vehicles here!

Sketch your gadgets here!

Personal gadgets can also be useful to your character. Think of something that would help your character achieve their goal, then turn it into a gadget! Maybe a high-tech phone or watch that projects holograms?

Sketch your accessories here!

Accessories can range from a scrunchie to a sword. They are usually pretty personal to the character, so figure out which item would match them best. A magic wand or a hat? An ancient amulet? Rings? All four?

Imagine and Sketch Your Villain or Conflict

Your story might not even have a true villain. Your villain could be a friendly rival, a bratty sibling, or a mean dog that chases you to and from school.

However, if you do have a true villain, you should explore how they came to be by developing their own backstory. Villains usually represent what the hero isn't.

They sometimes have a similar goal but go about it in very different ways. A good villain should be able to challenge the hero to find new ways to defeat them.

And make sure they look really good! Manga villains always shop high-end.

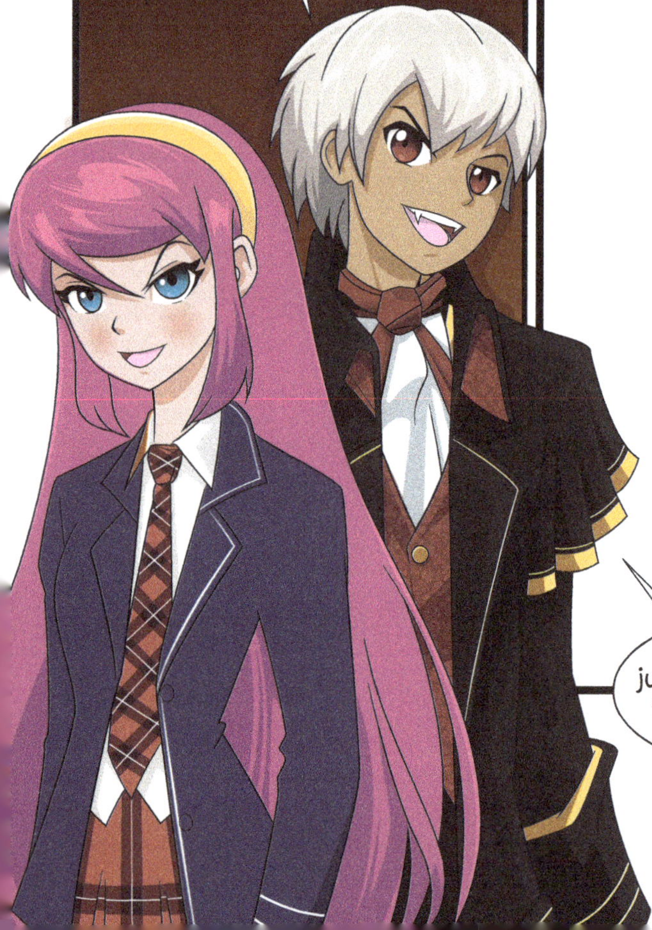

Or you could just choose a conflict the character must figure out.

Conflict can be that test you need to pass to get an A in class, self-doubt, or maybe an alien invasion. This can be emotional and physical. You'll need to know how to identify the conflict and what is needed to resolve it.

Sketch your villain here!

Outline and Write Your Story

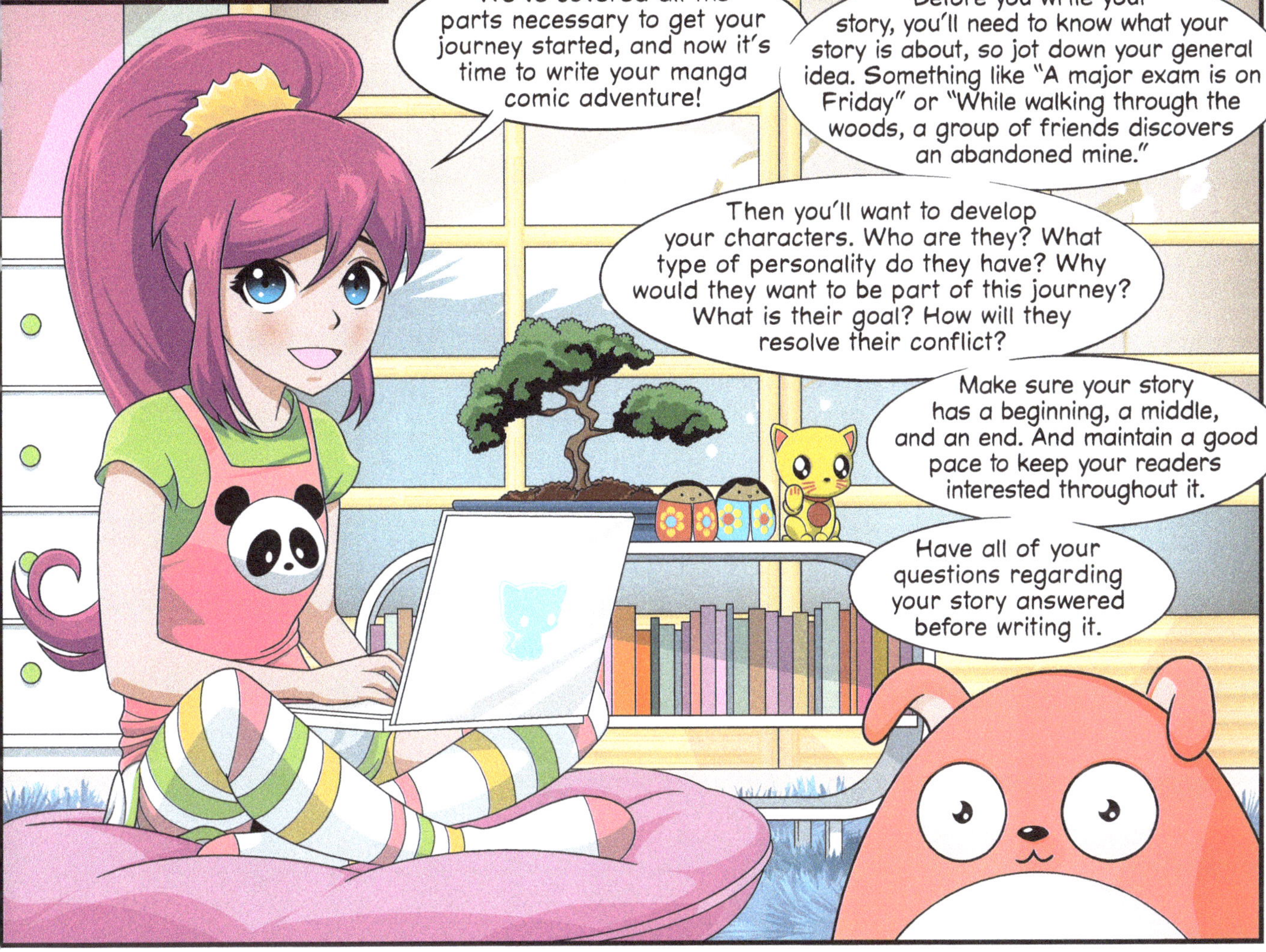
We've covered all the parts necessary to get your journey started, and now it's time to write your manga comic adventure!
Before you write your story, you'll need to know what your story is about, so jot down your general idea. Something like "A major exam is on Friday" or "While walking through the woods, a group of friends discovers an abandoned mine."
Then you'll want to develop your characters. Who are they? What type of personality do they have? Why would they want to be part of this journey? What is their goal? How will they resolve their conflict?
Make sure your story has a beginning, a middle, and an end. And maintain a good pace to keep your readers interested throughout it.
Have all of your questions regarding your story answered before writing it.

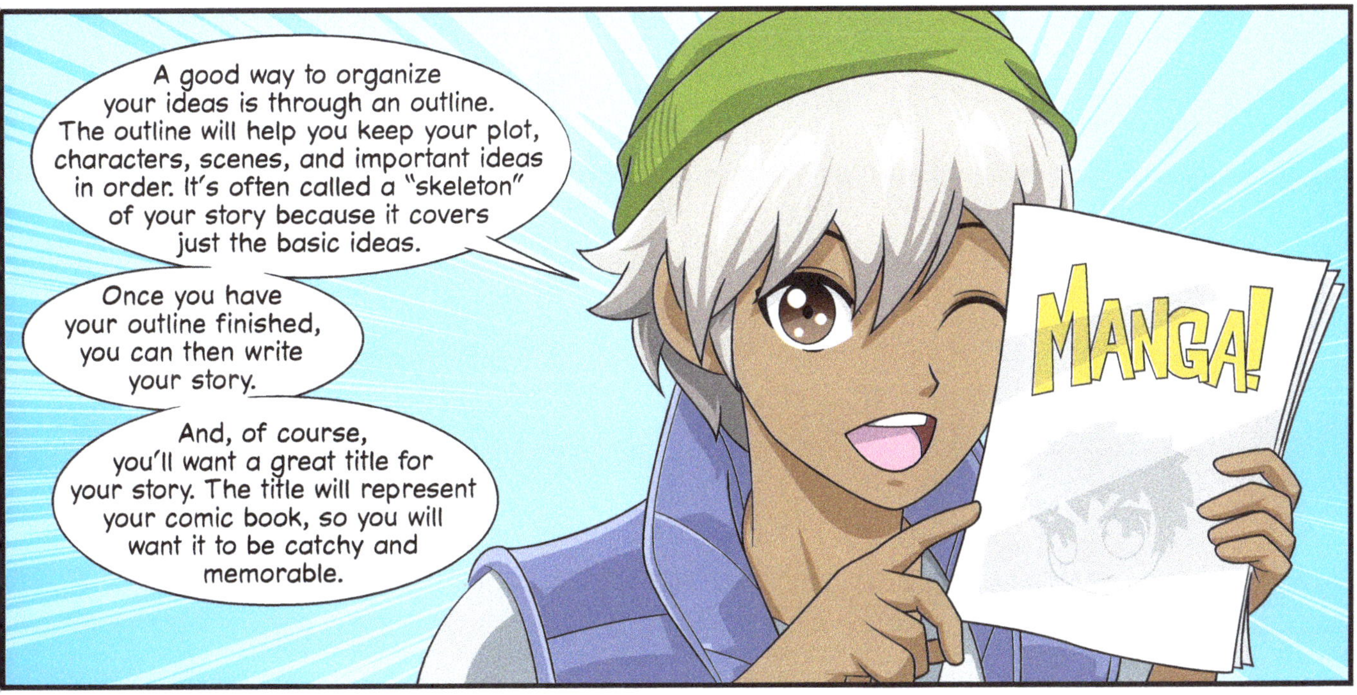
A good way to organize your ideas is through an outline. The outline will help you keep your plot, characters, scenes, and important ideas in order. It's often called a "skeleton" of your story because it covers just the basic ideas.
Once you have your outline finished, you can then write your story.
And, of course, you'll want a great title for your story. The title will represent your comic book, so you will want it to be catchy and memorable.
MANGA!

Plan Your Panels

In Japan, comics are read right to left, top to bottom, as shown in the diagram to the far right. You can choose to do the same, but it might be a bit confusing to your readers.

Panel spacing is also a bit different in manga comics than in American comics. With manga comics, the vertical spacing between the panels is narrower than the horizontal spacing (see diagram). This allows the eye to move more easily from one panel to the other.

Larger panels on a page are used to express more impactful moments like dramatic or action shots.

How to Read Manga Comic Book Panels

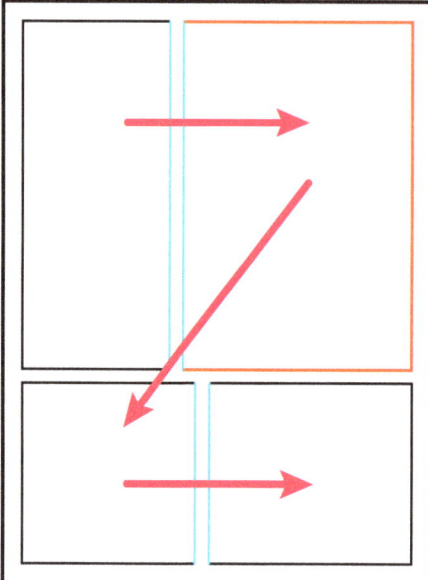

American Comic Book 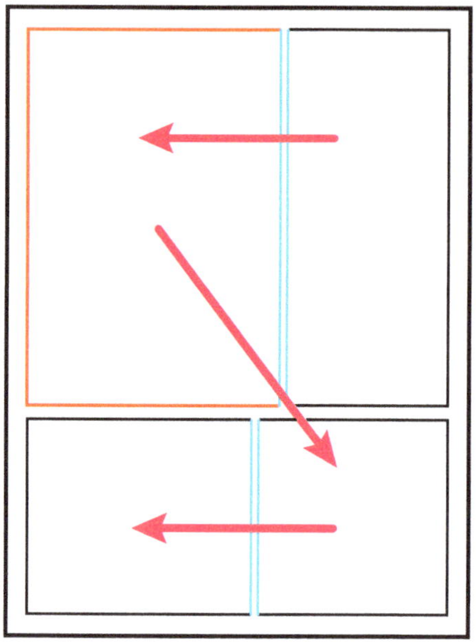   *Japanese Manga Comic*

When laying out your comic pages, you may want to first draw thumbnails of them. Thumbnails are simple sketches that help you map out your comic book pages. They should be rough and quick. See the example below.

These should be done on a separate piece of paper.

Visual pacing is key to manga storytelling. You'll need to keep a good panel-to-panel flow so your audience can follow the story before you even add text.

Background elements—such as buildings and the use of negative space, or the areas around and between the characters—can be great for keeping the flow.

The characters' movements and gestures are also great for moving the eye from panel to panel.

Motion lines are also used as a background element for action scenes to give the panel a sense of movement.

Sketch Out Your Story

Dialogue Balloons, Thought Balloons, and Sound Effects (SFX)

Dialogue balloons contain your characters' conversations. They can be stylized to fit the character speaking.
Thought balloons are used for nonverbal dialogue, when the character is thinking.

Sketch dialogue balloons here!

Sketch thought balloons here!

Sound effects can add impact to a page. Remember this is a comic book, so you will have to visually show sound.
A BOOM! could give the right visual pop to an explosion, or a soft PURRRRR could show a happy cat.
Mew?

Sketch sound effects (SFX) here!

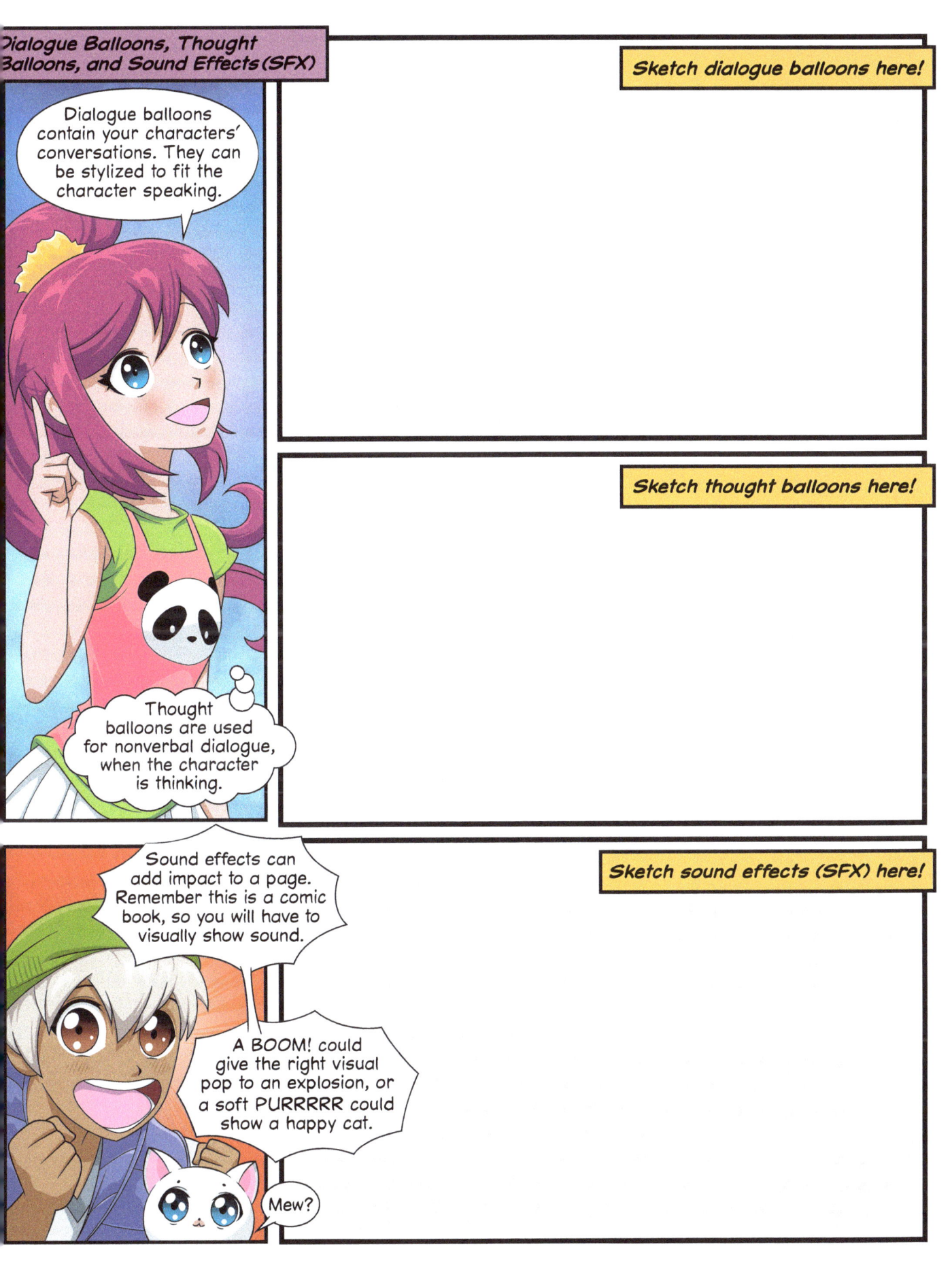

Lettering

The letterer writes the text in the word balloons. The letterer also draws the visual effects.

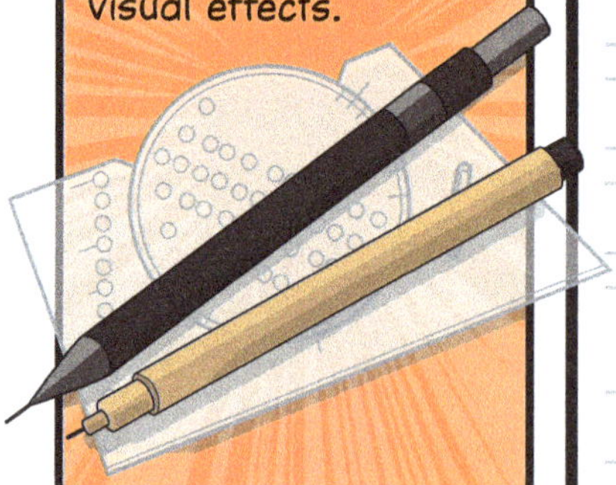

Practice your lettering here.

MANGA

Inking

Inking is going over your pencil lines with black ink to create a bolder, higher-contrast image.

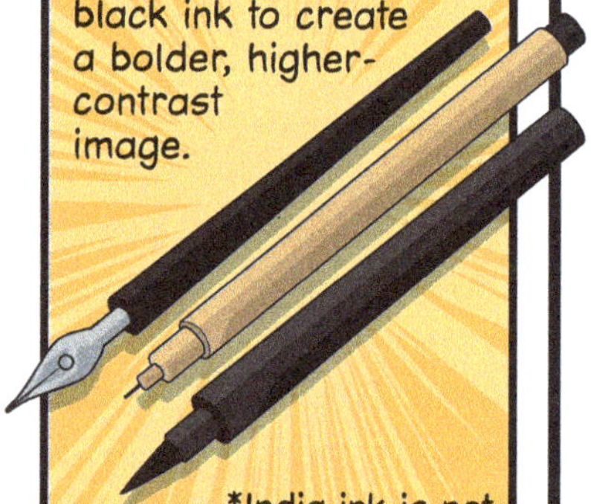

*India ink is not recommended, as it may bleed through the paper.

Draw your character, ink it, then color it in.

Coloring

Manga comics are generally done in black and white. Black and white is great for expressing mood with hints of gray added for shading, but feel free to add color, as this is your book.

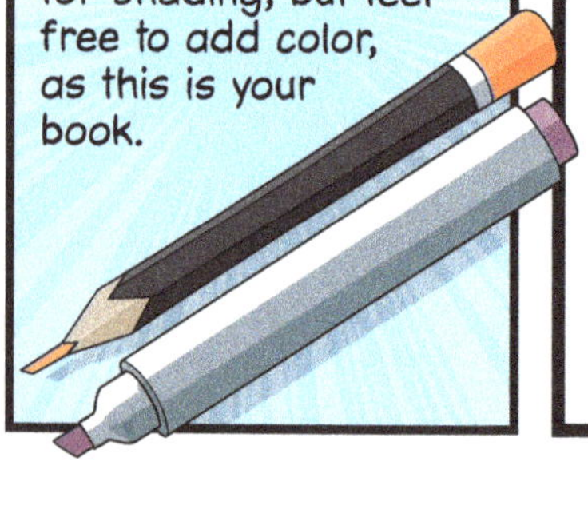

Design and Sketch Your Manga Cover

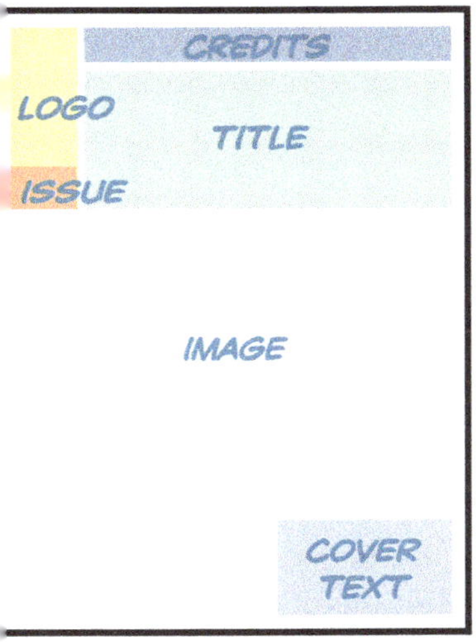
CREDITS
LOGO
TITLE
ISSUE
IMAGE
COVER TEXT

Sketch your cover here!

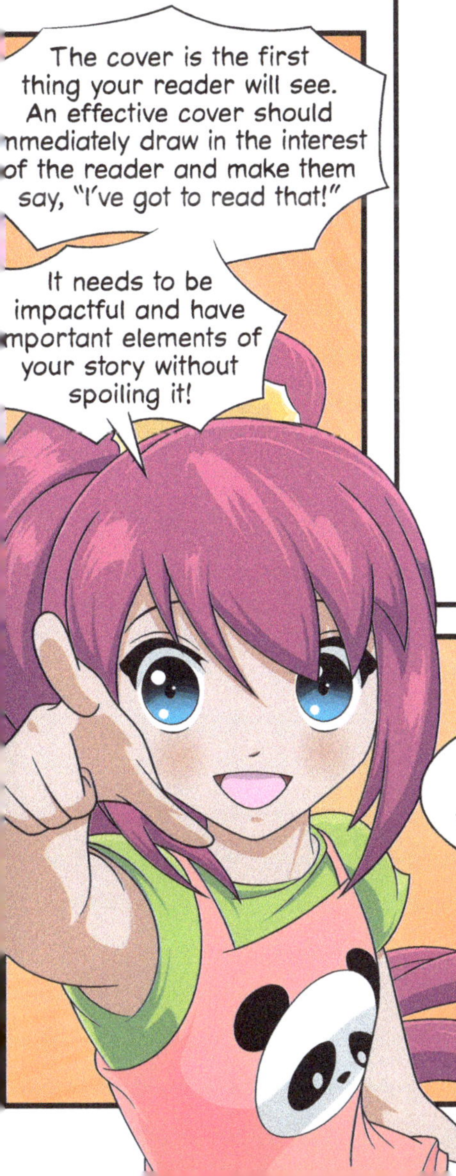
The cover is the first thing your reader will see. An effective cover should immediately draw in the interest of the reader and make them say, "I've got to read that!"
It needs to be impactful and have important elements of your story without spoiling it!

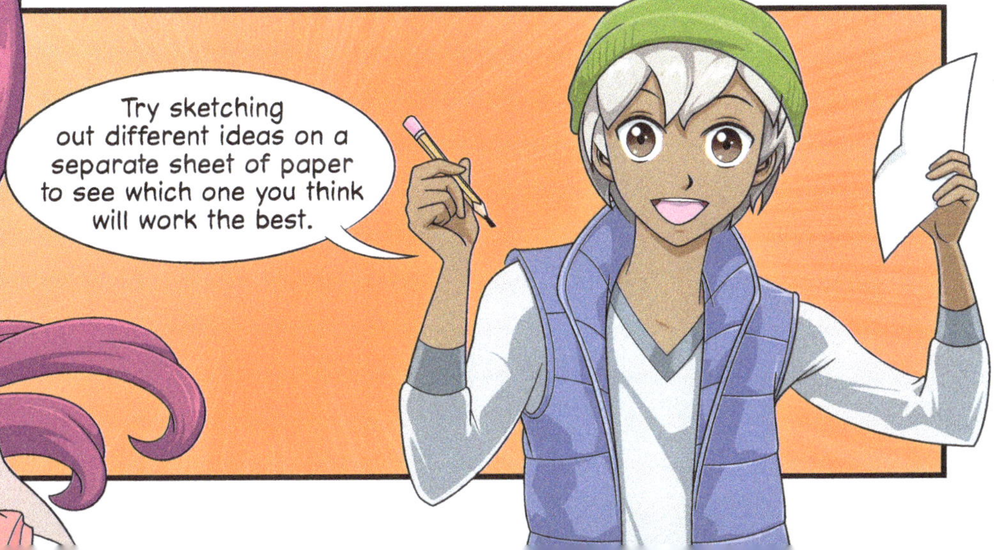
Try sketching out different ideas on a separate sheet of paper to see which one you think will work the best.

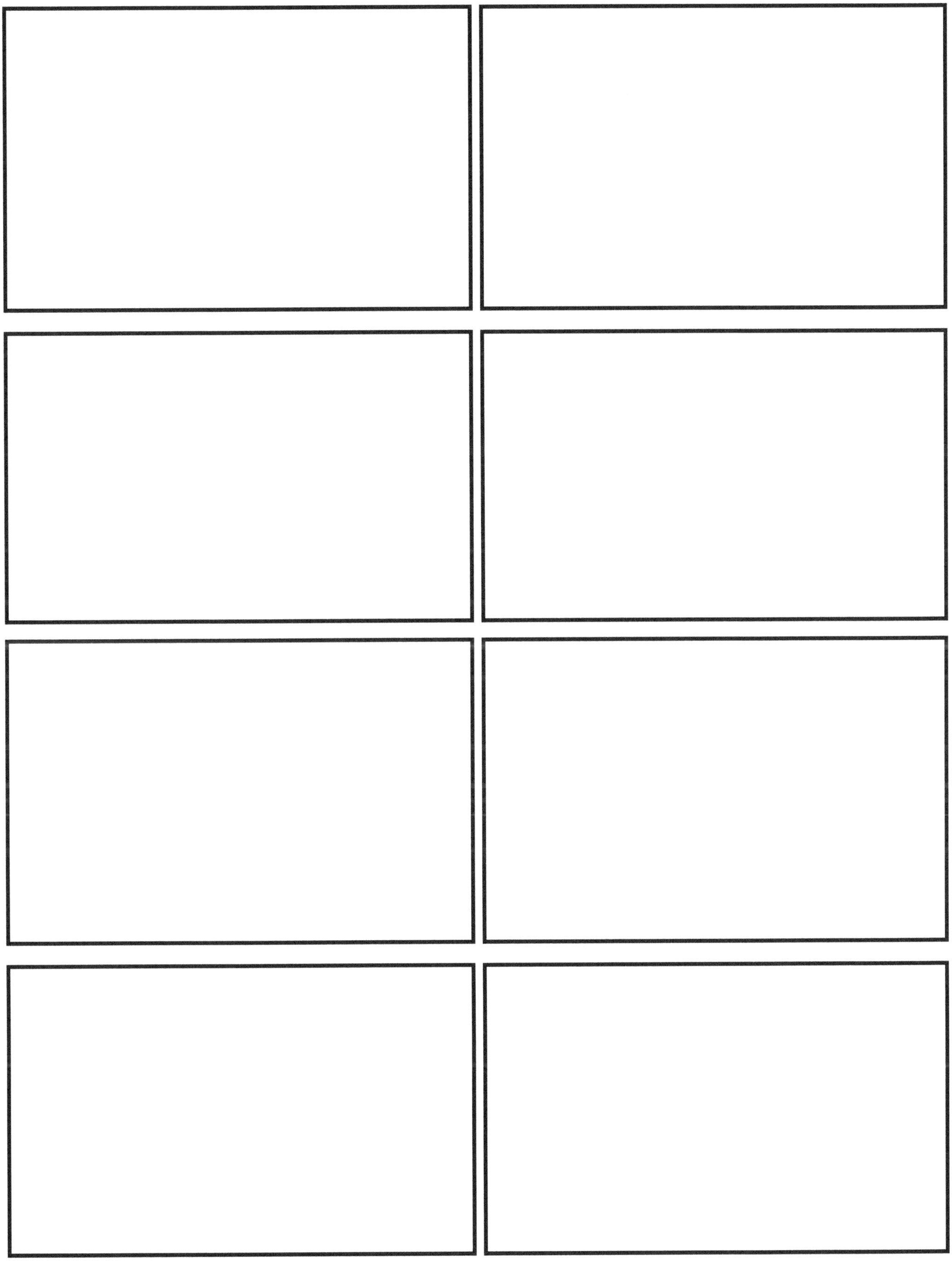

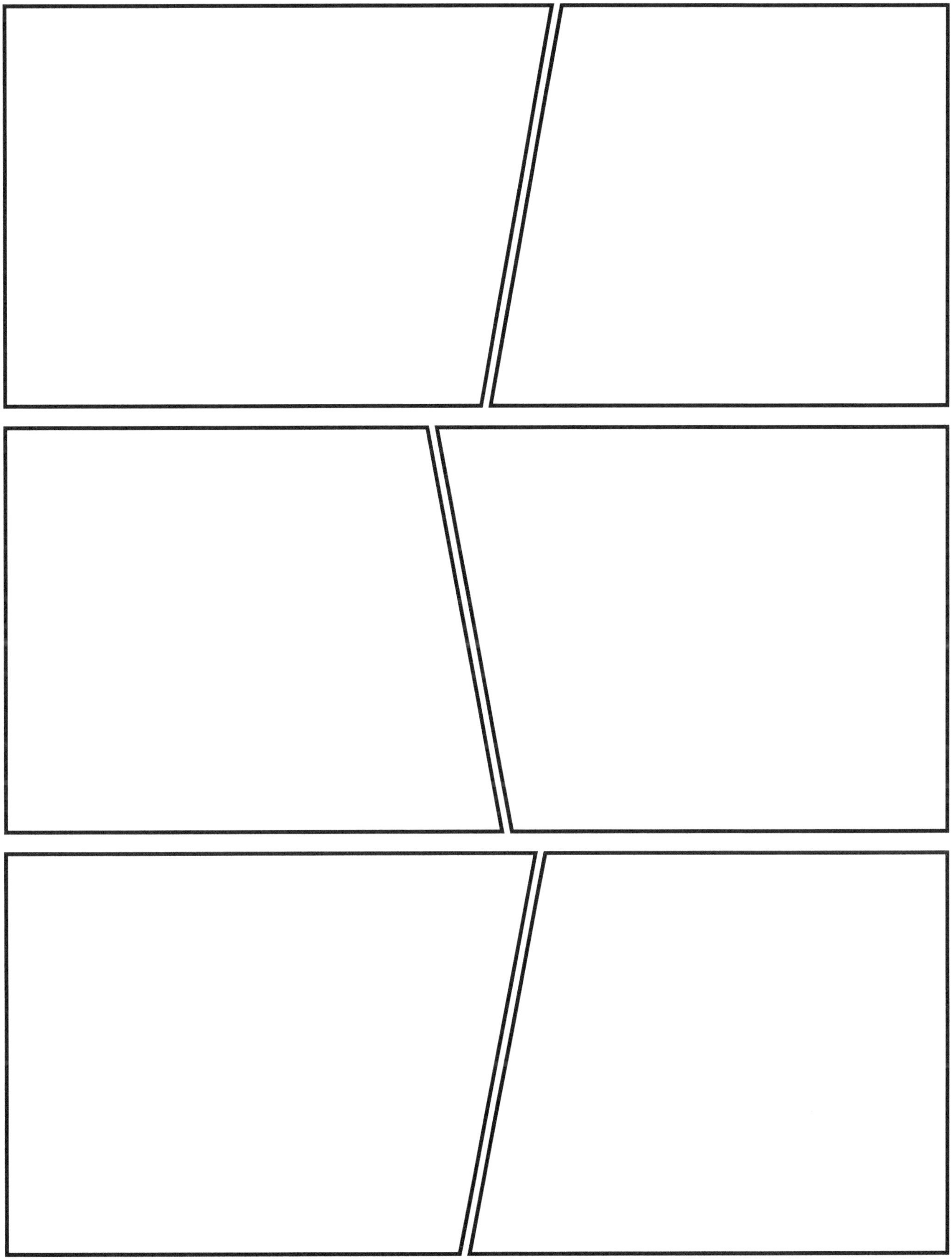

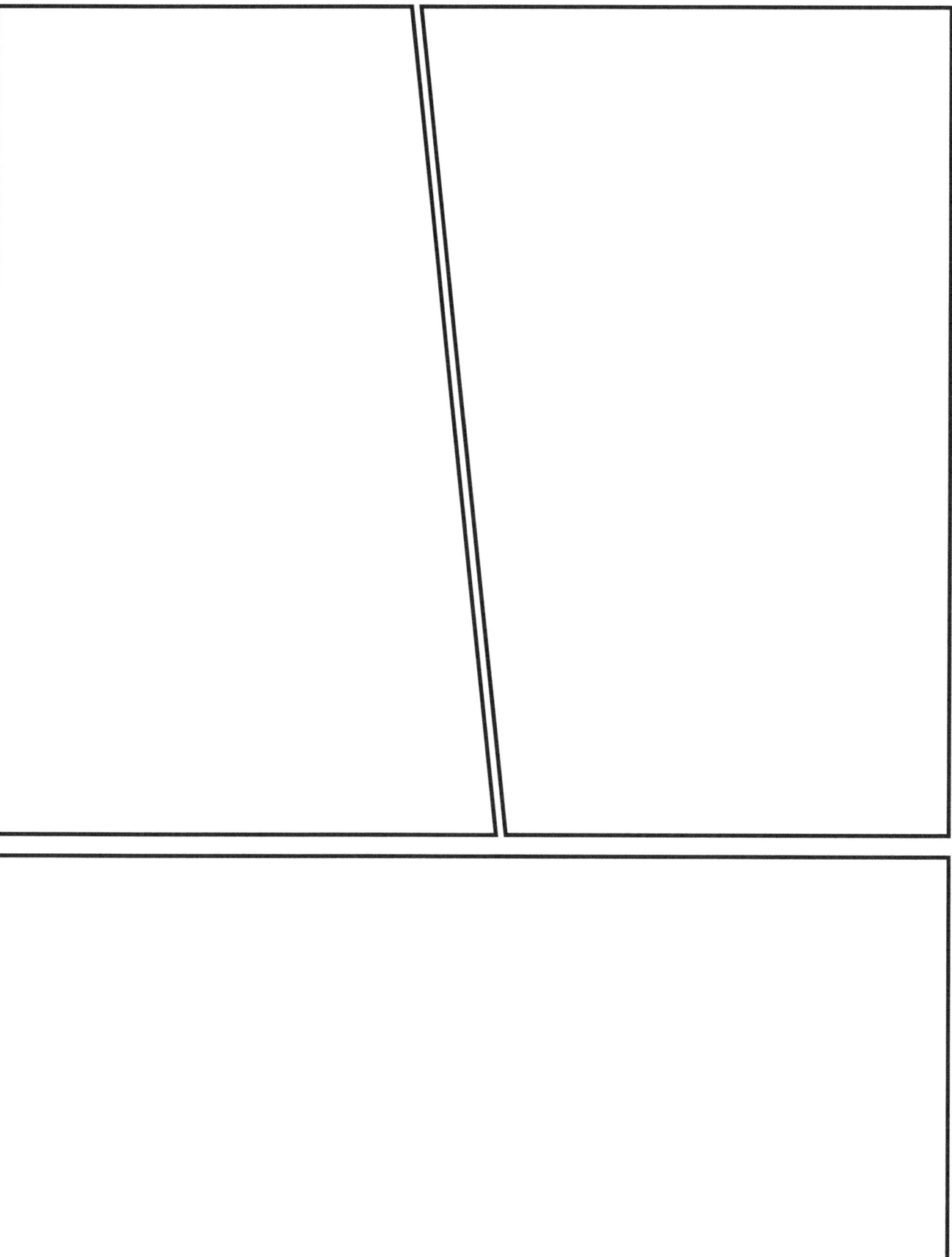

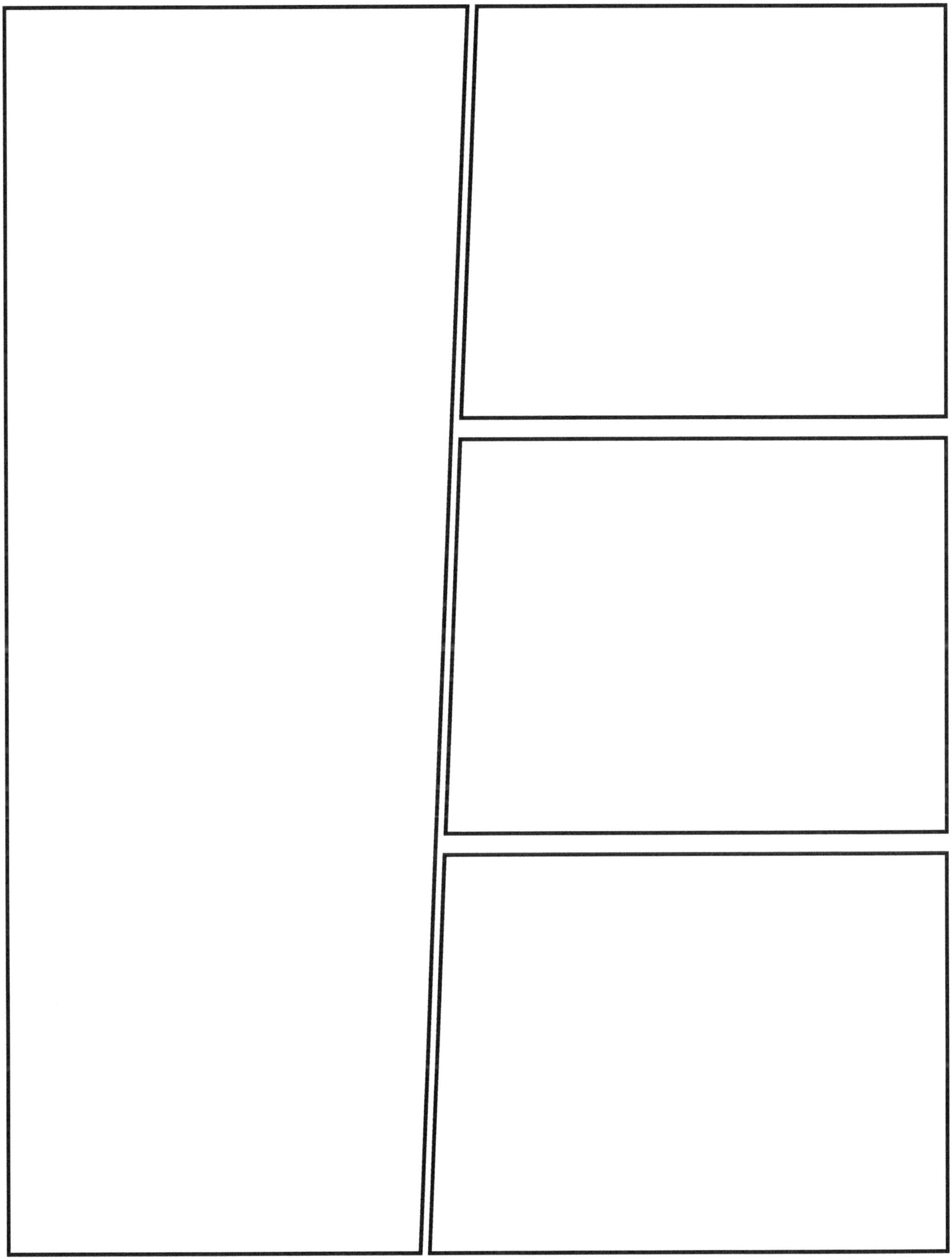

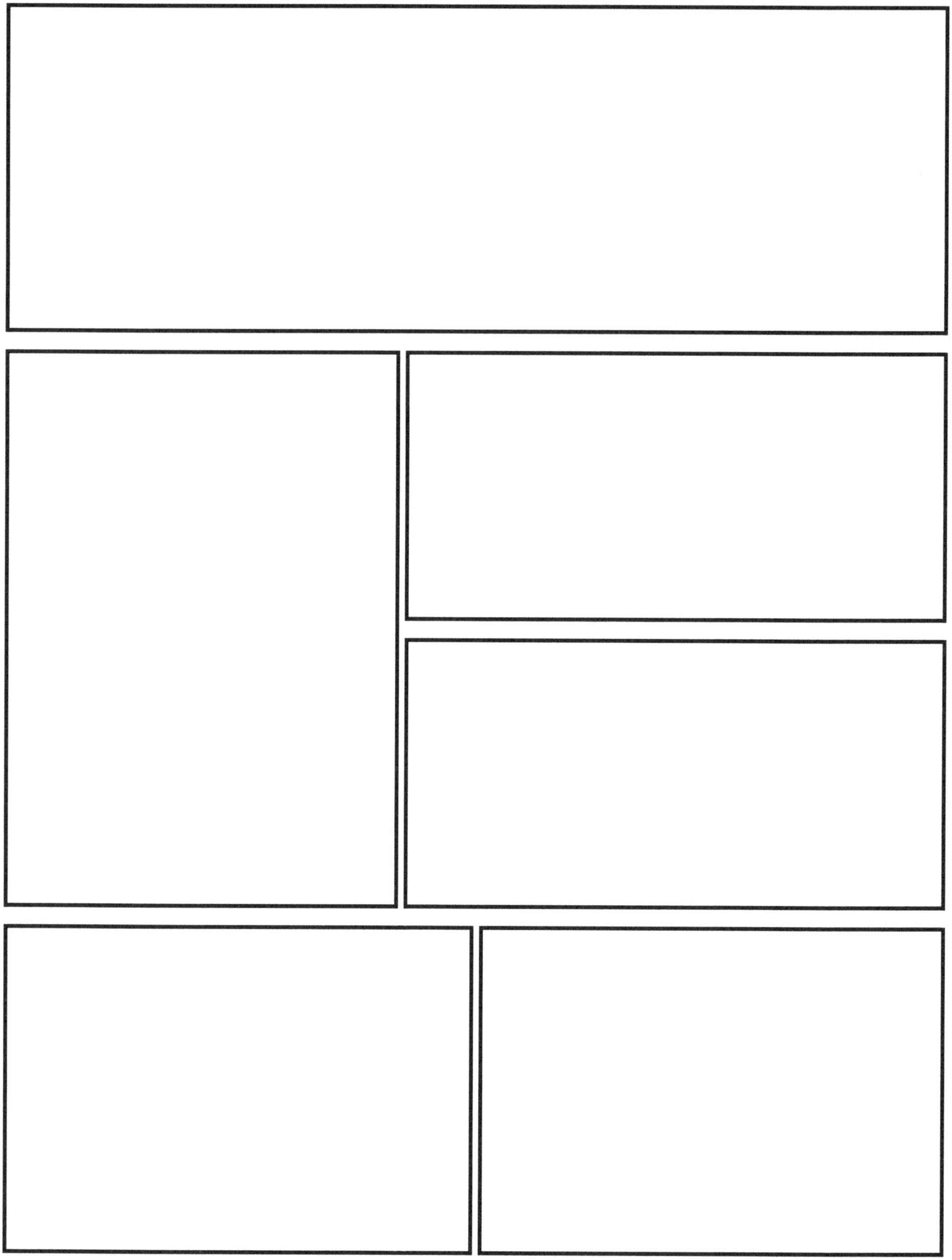

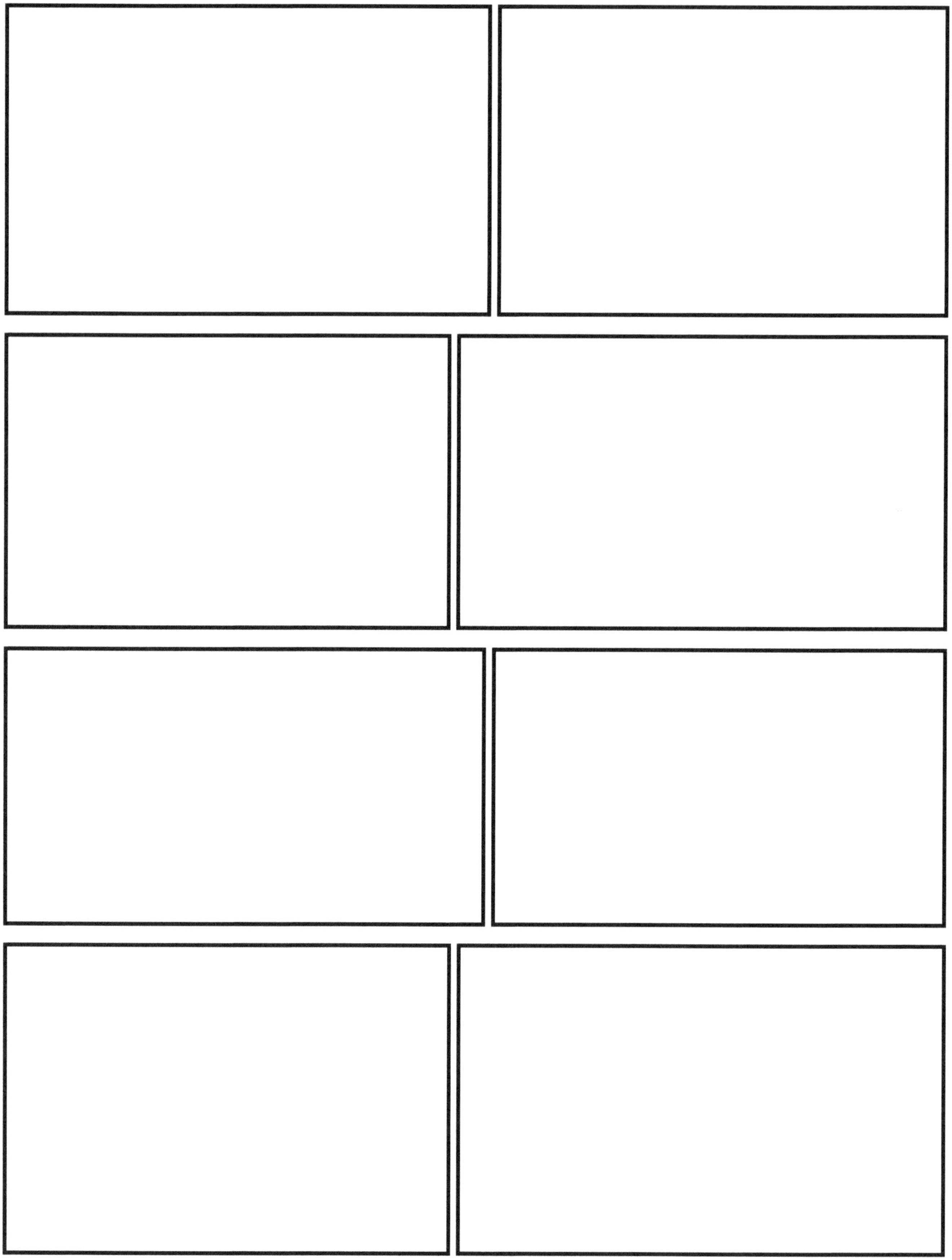

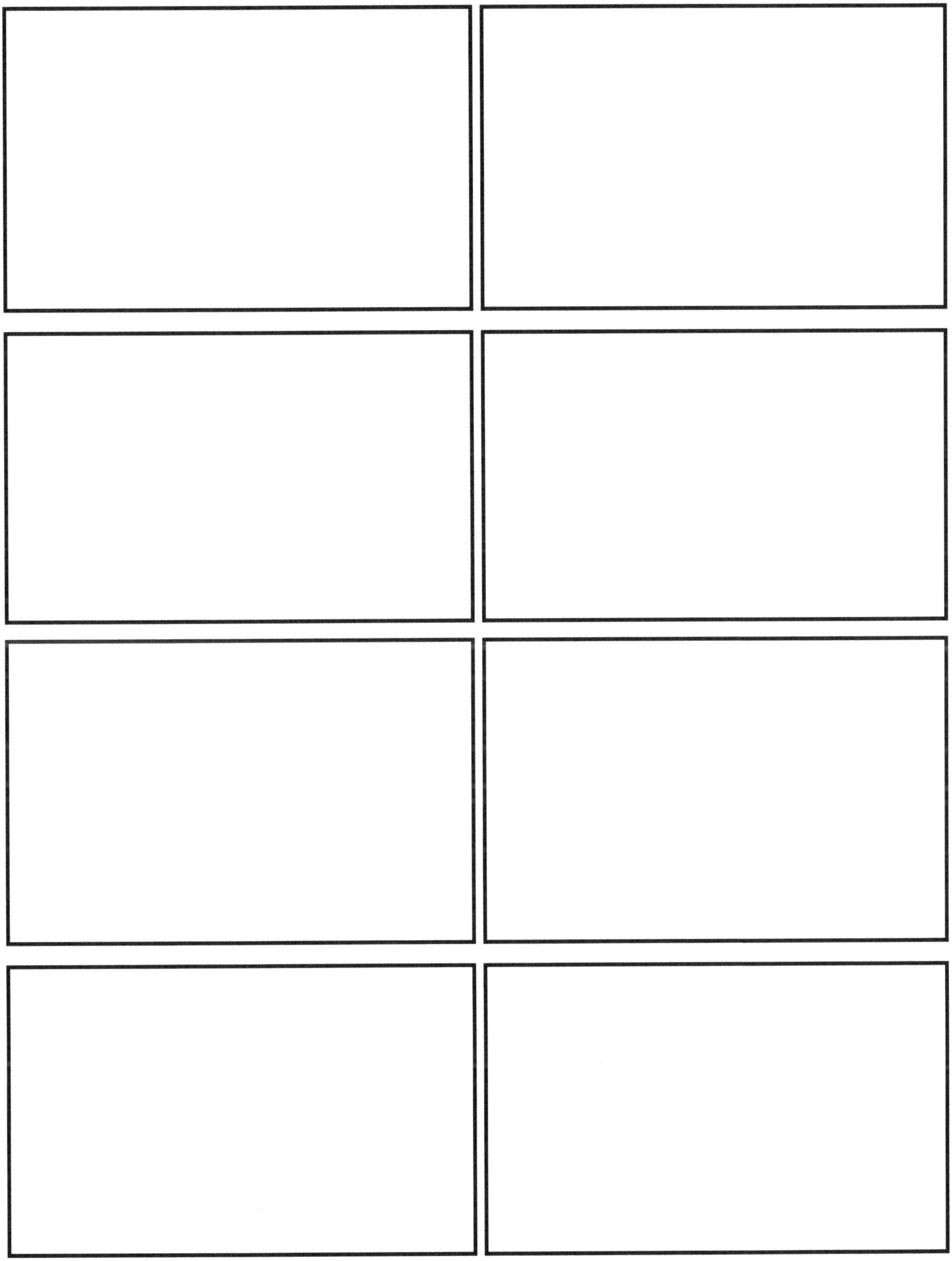

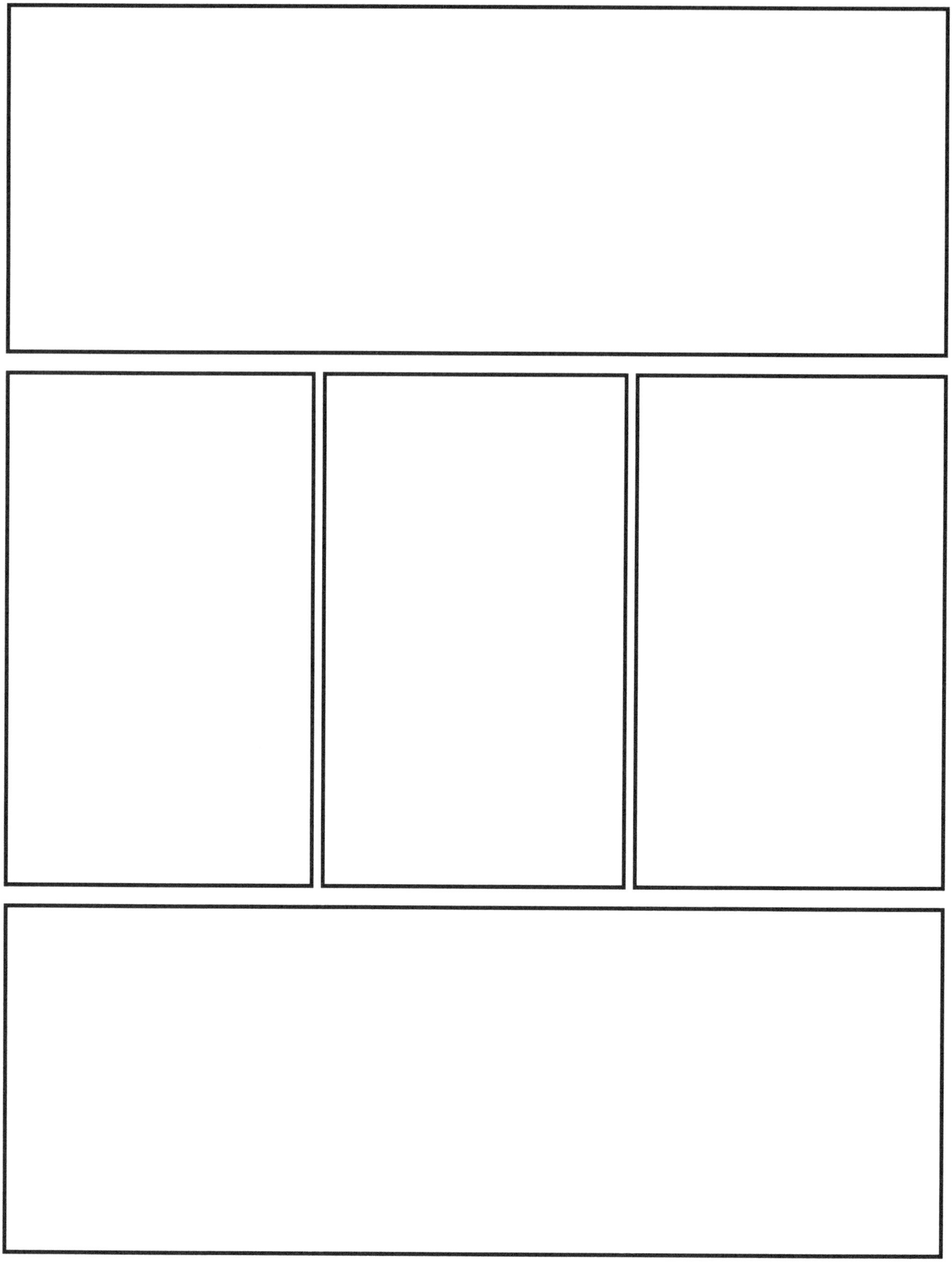

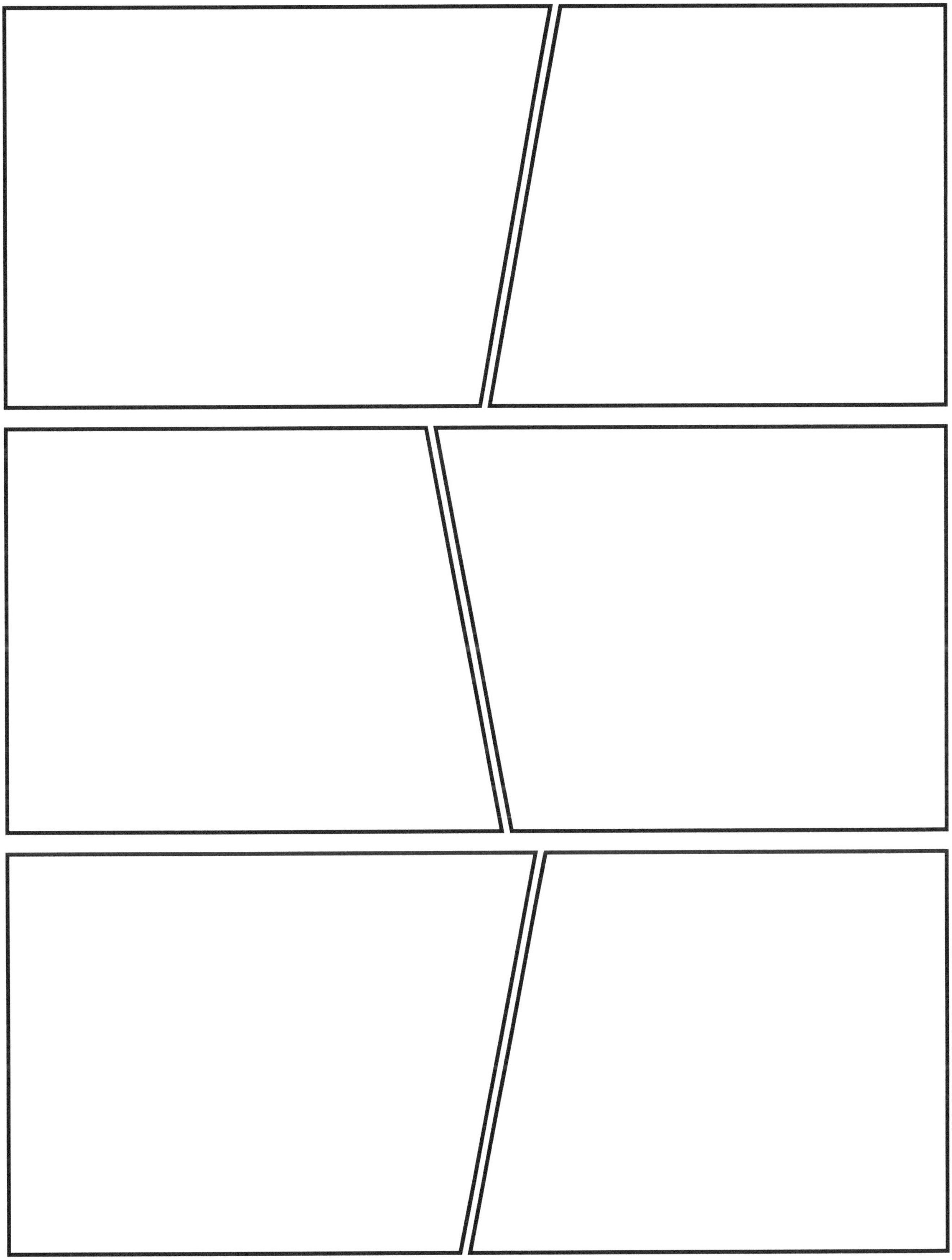

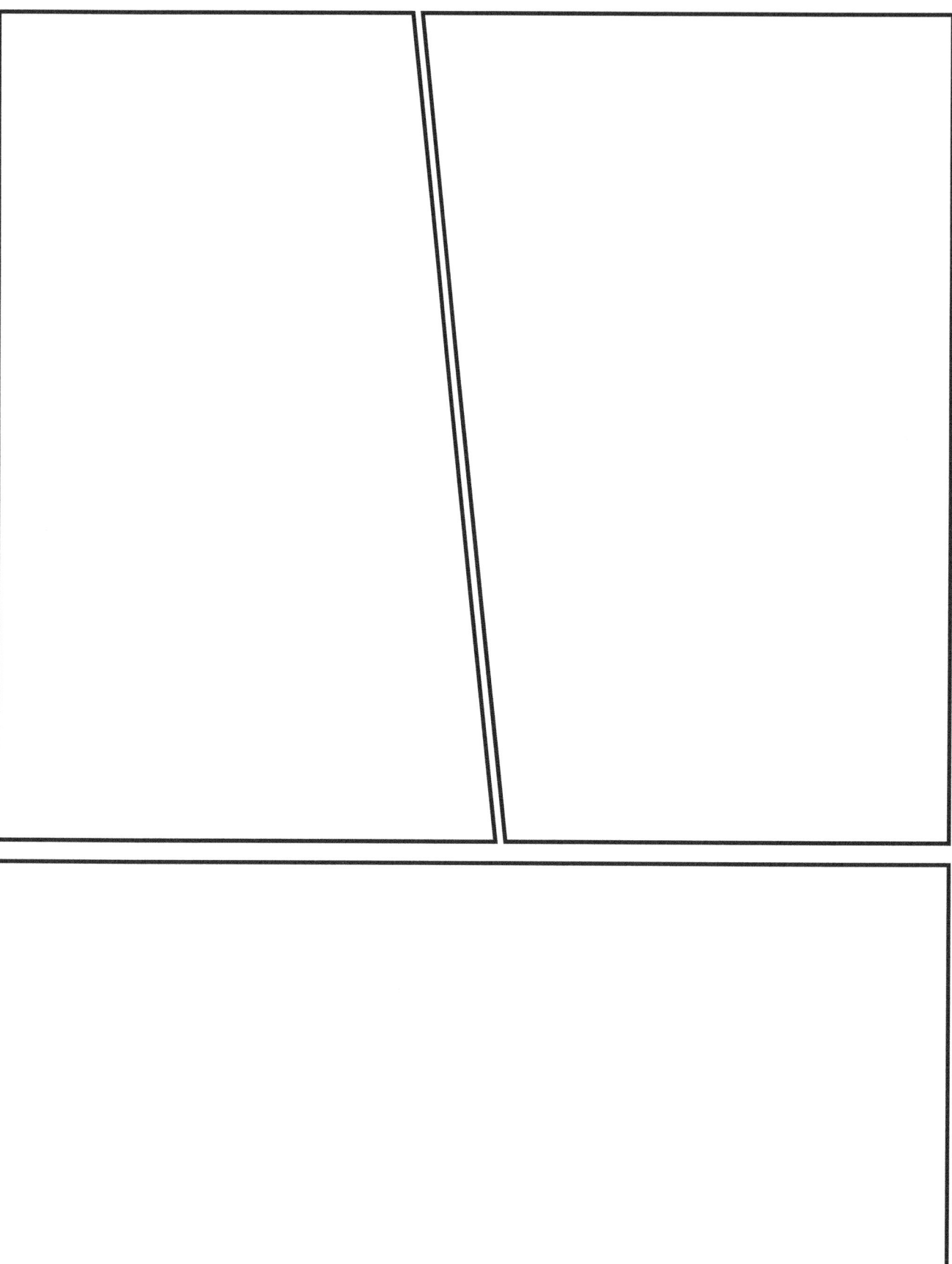

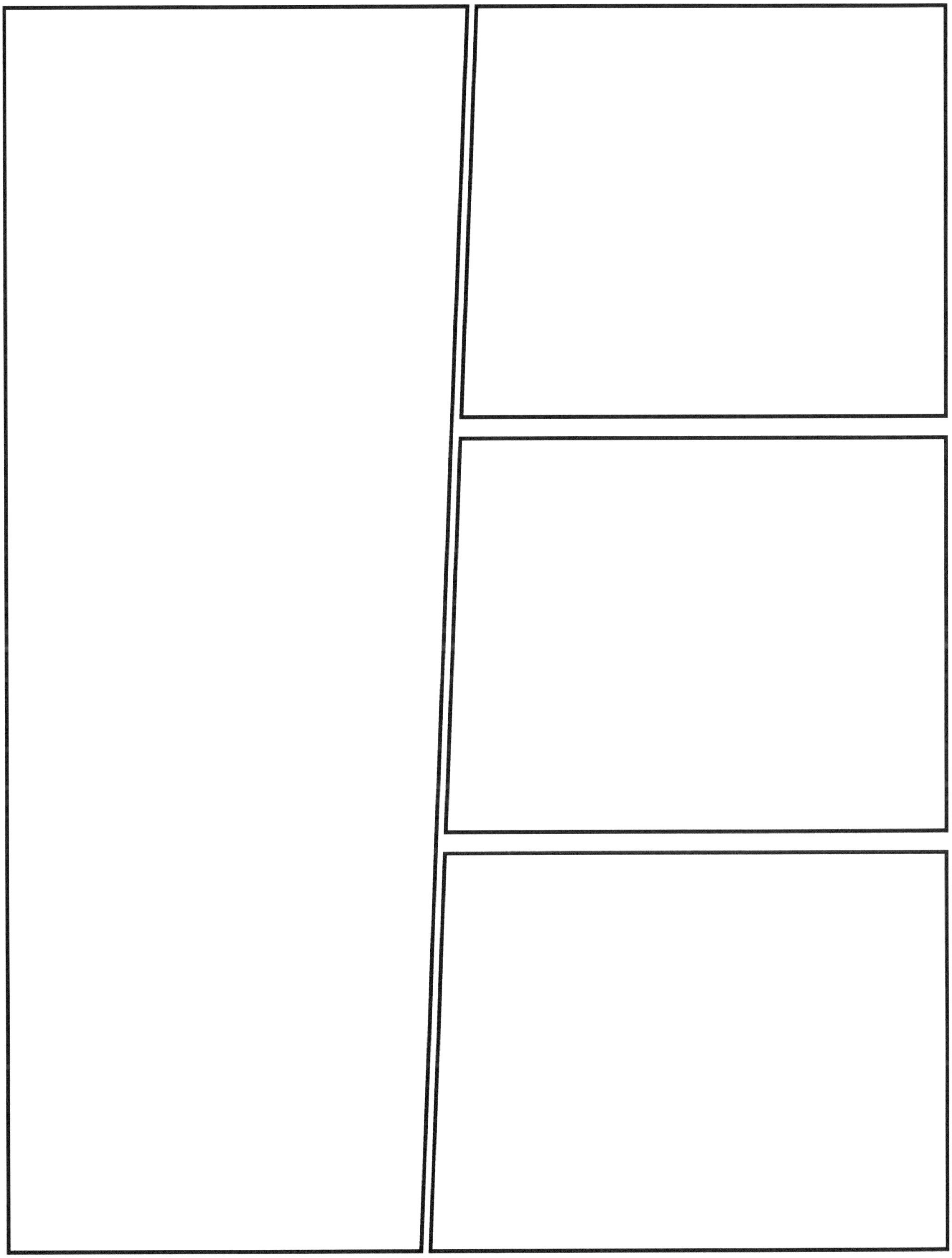

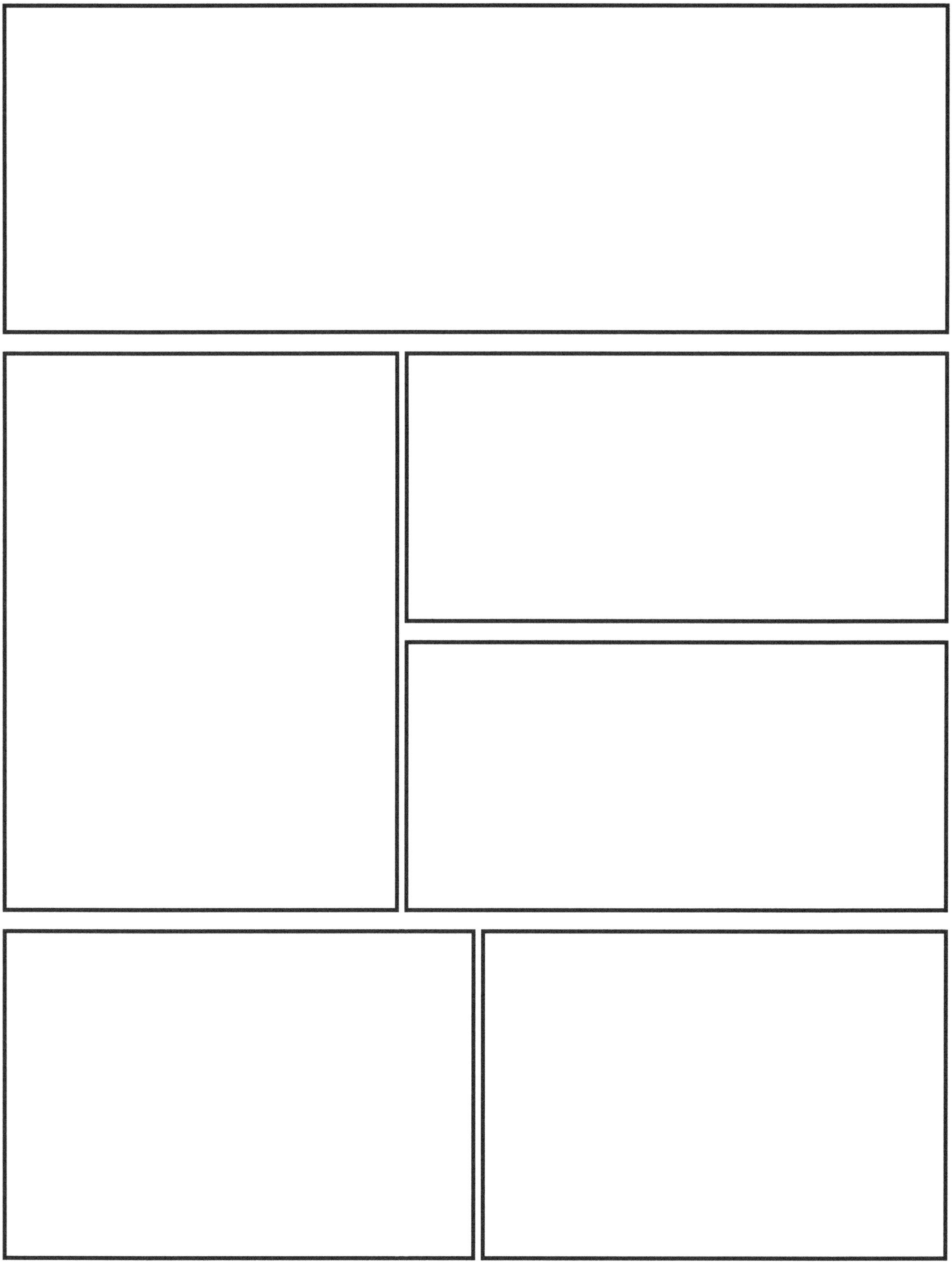

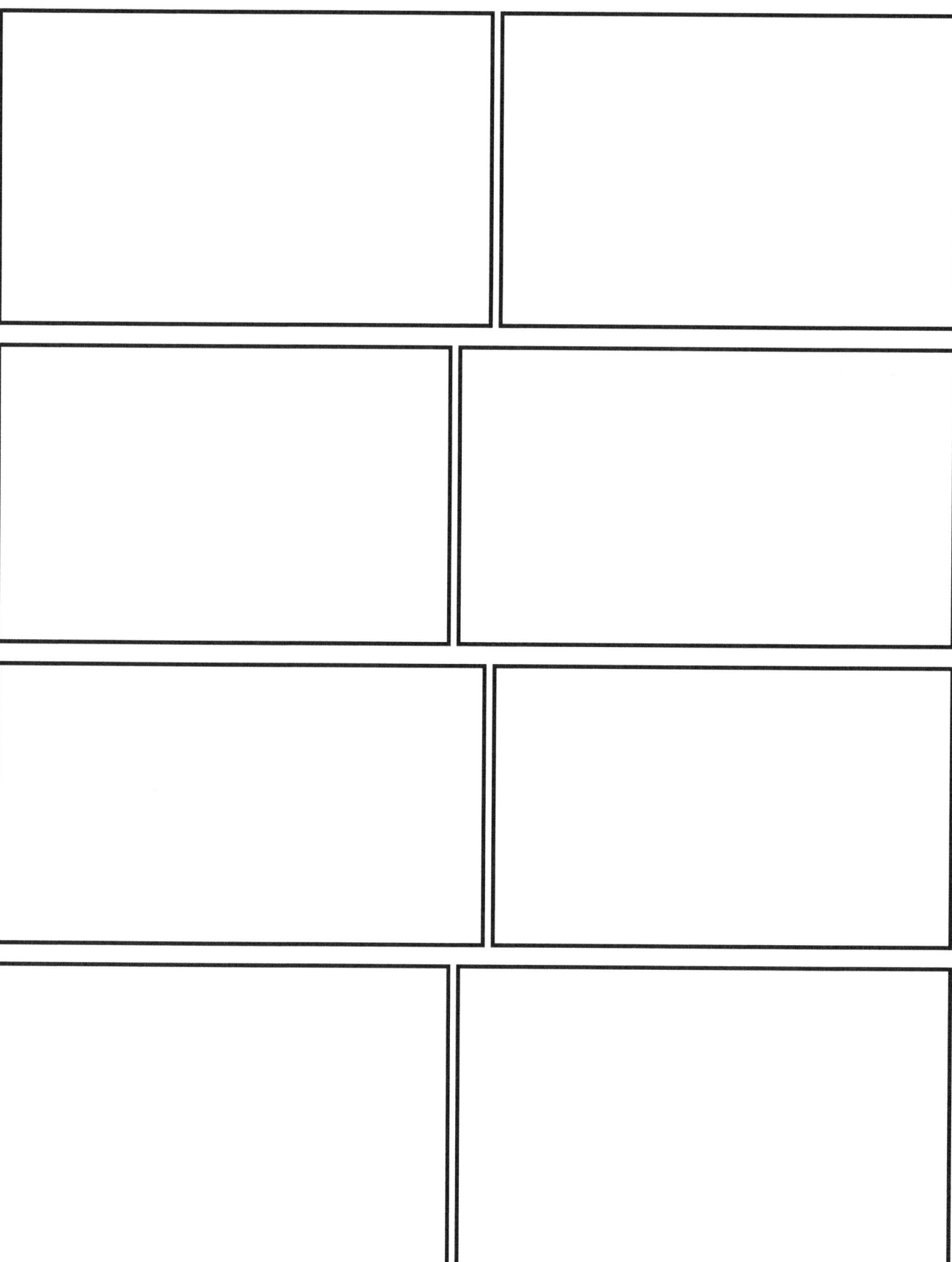

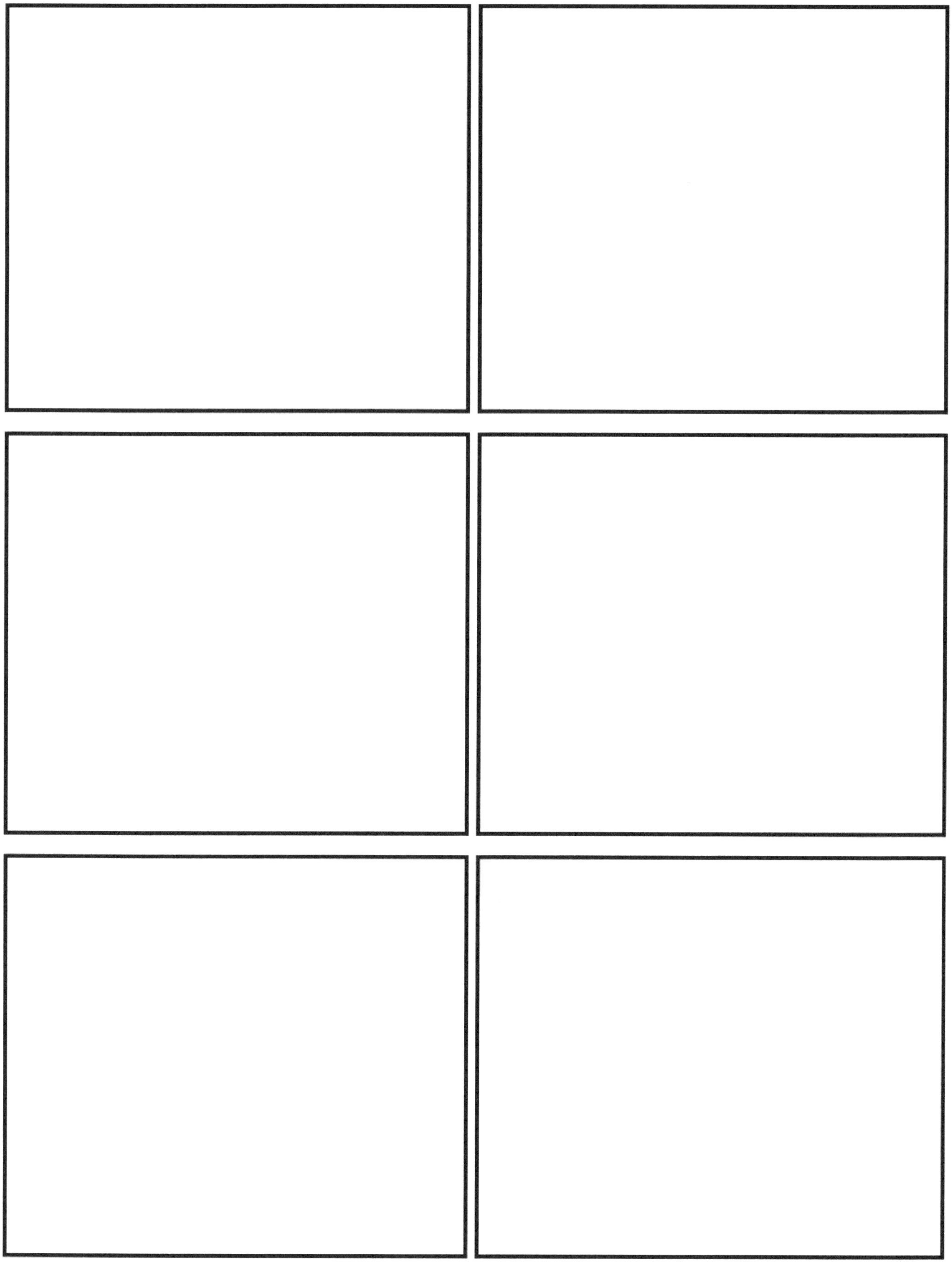

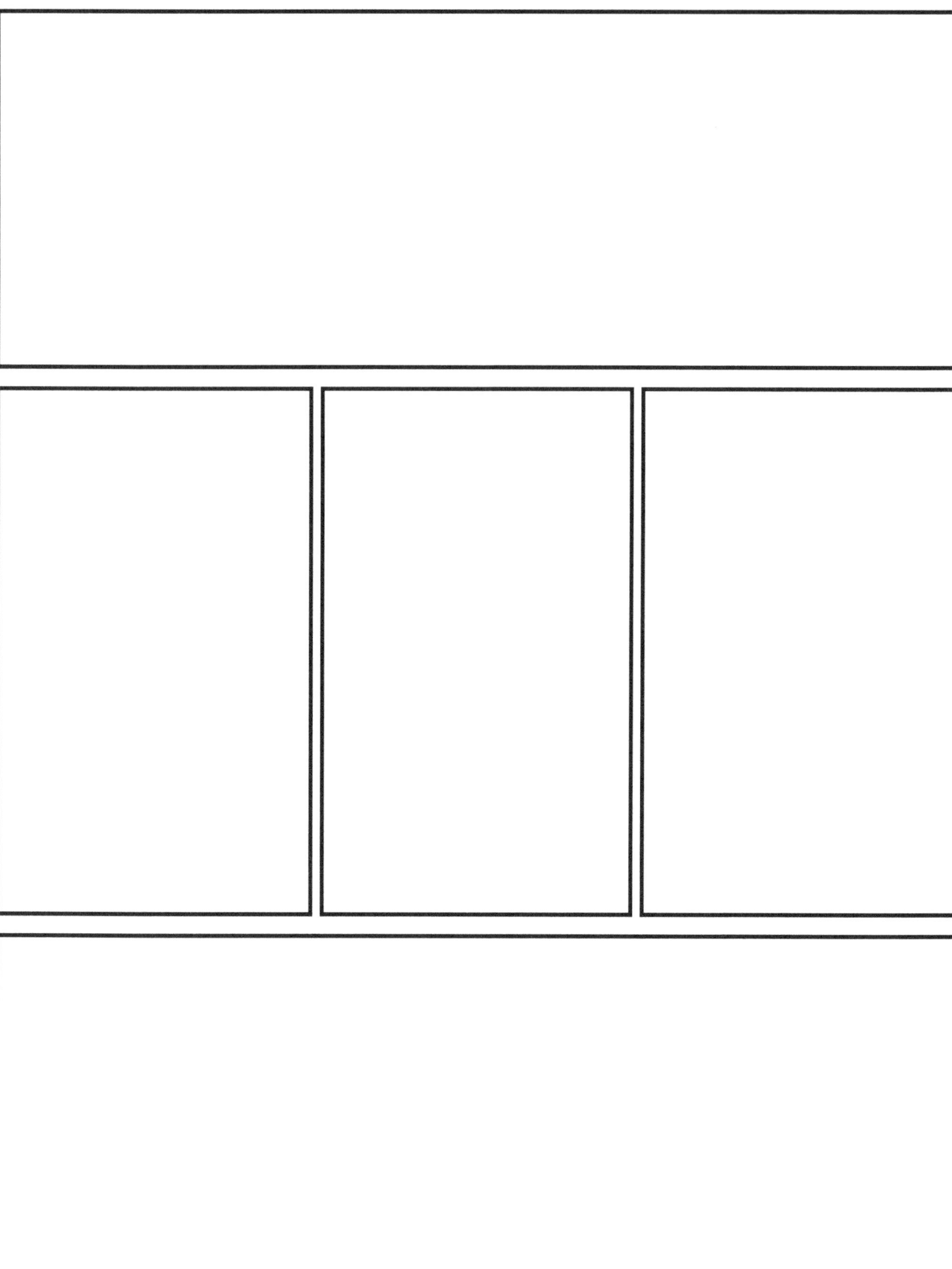

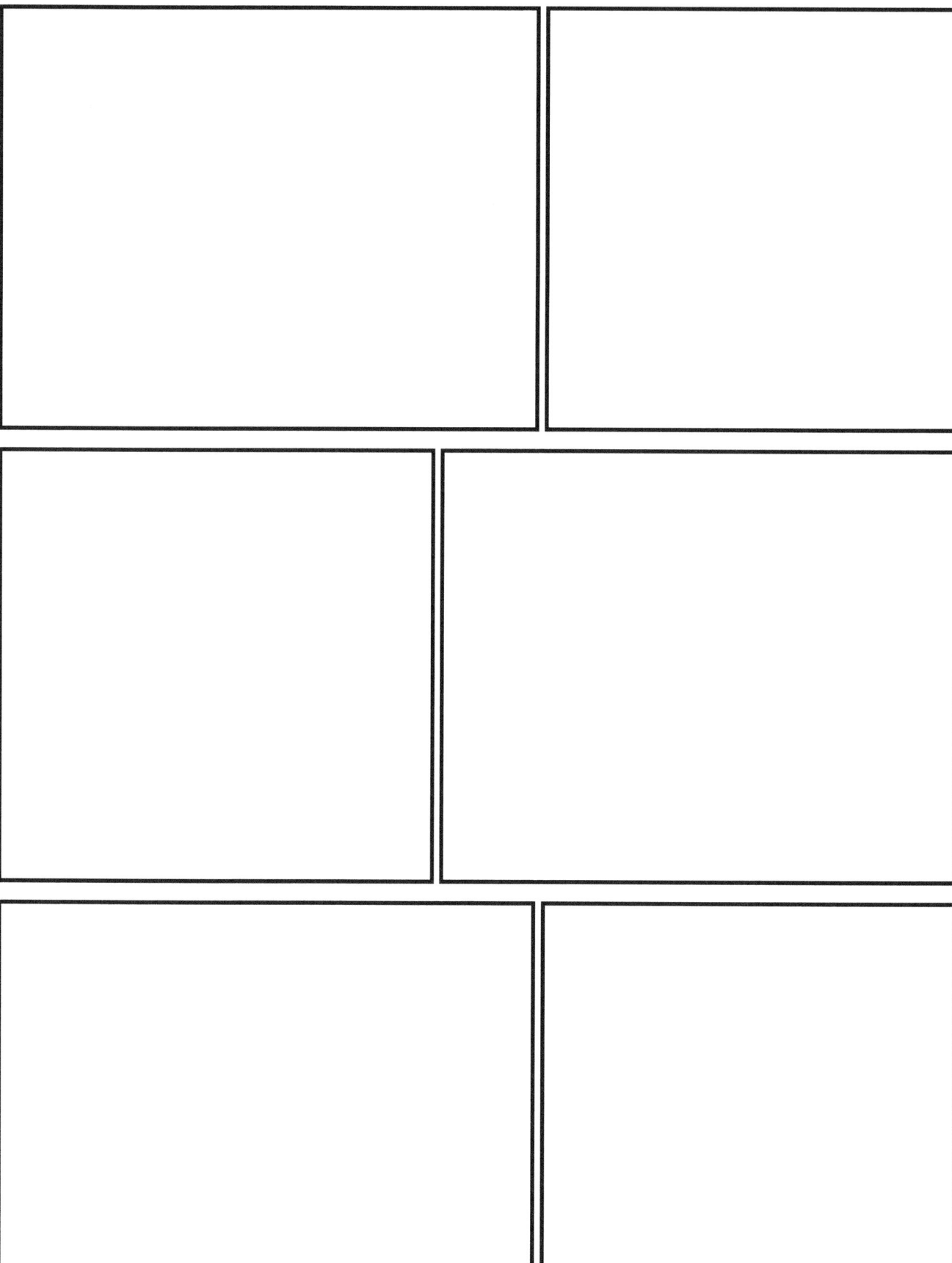

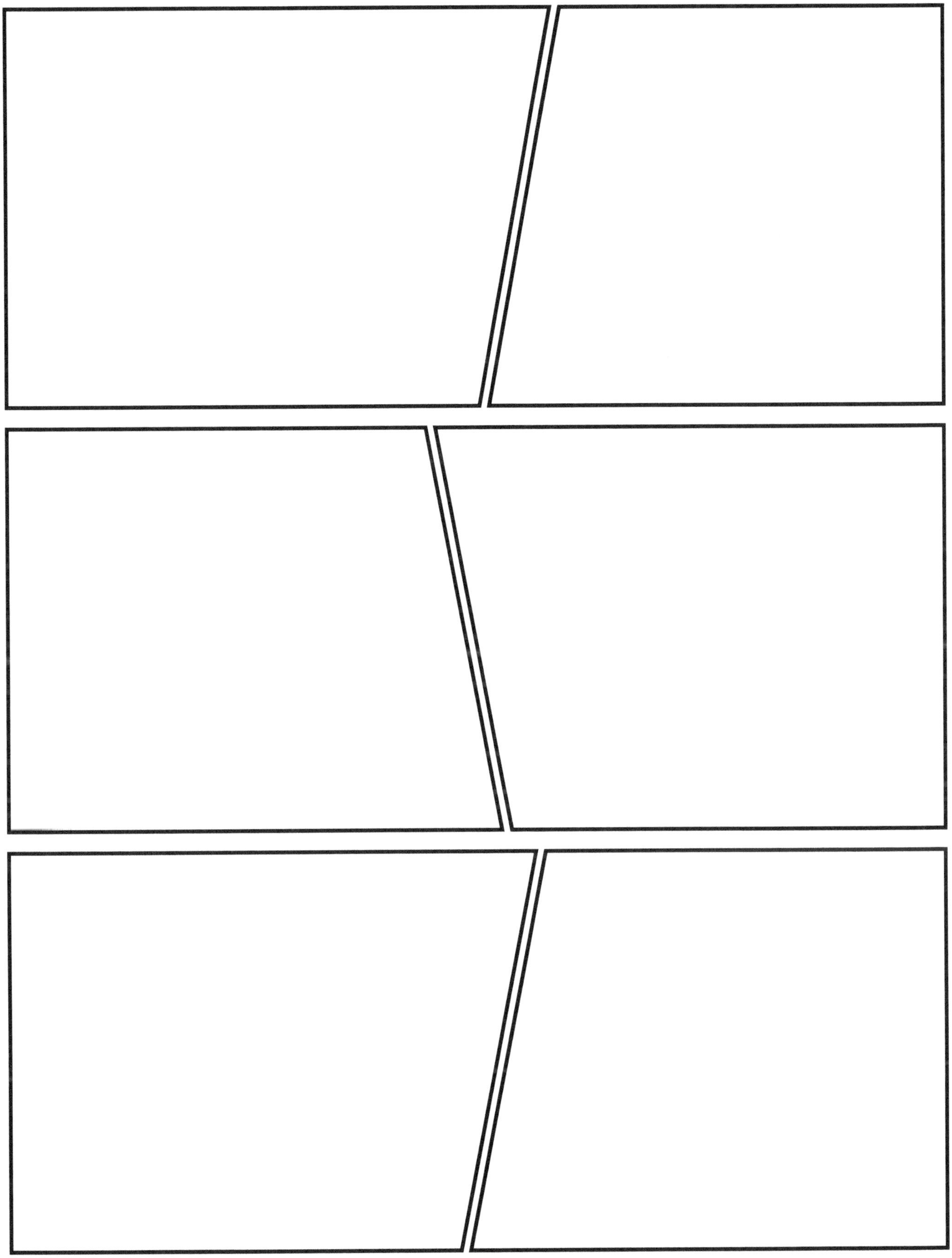

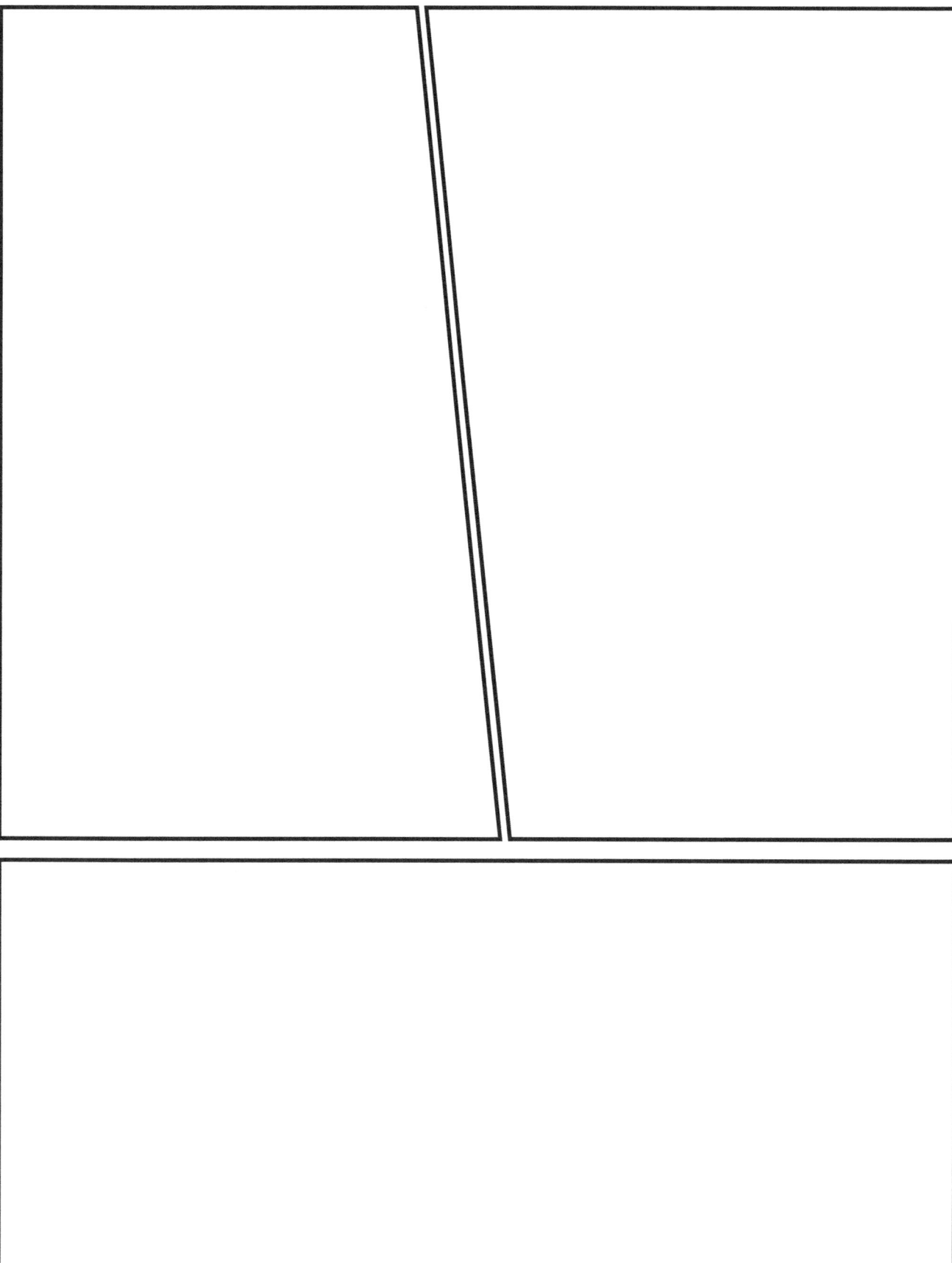

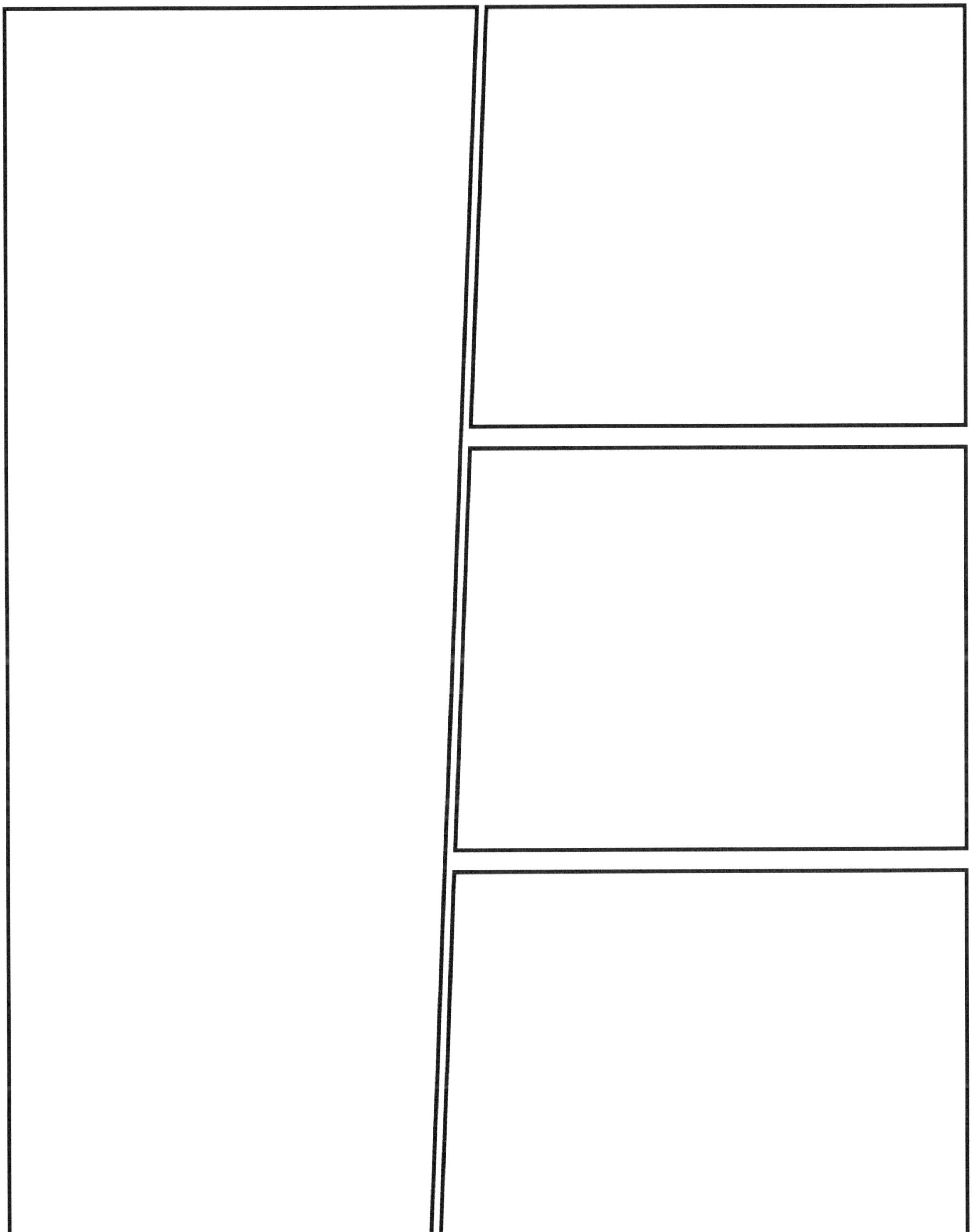

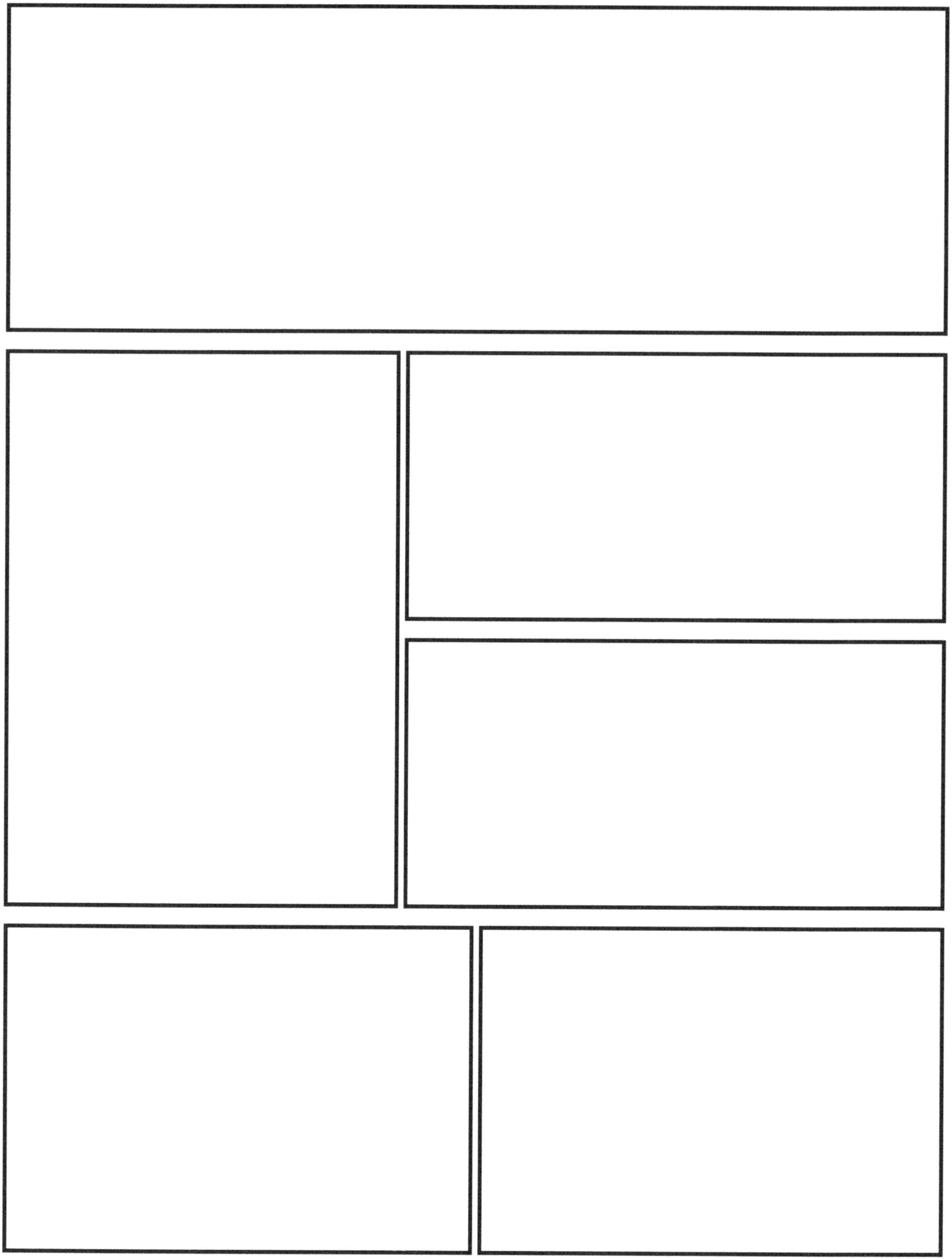

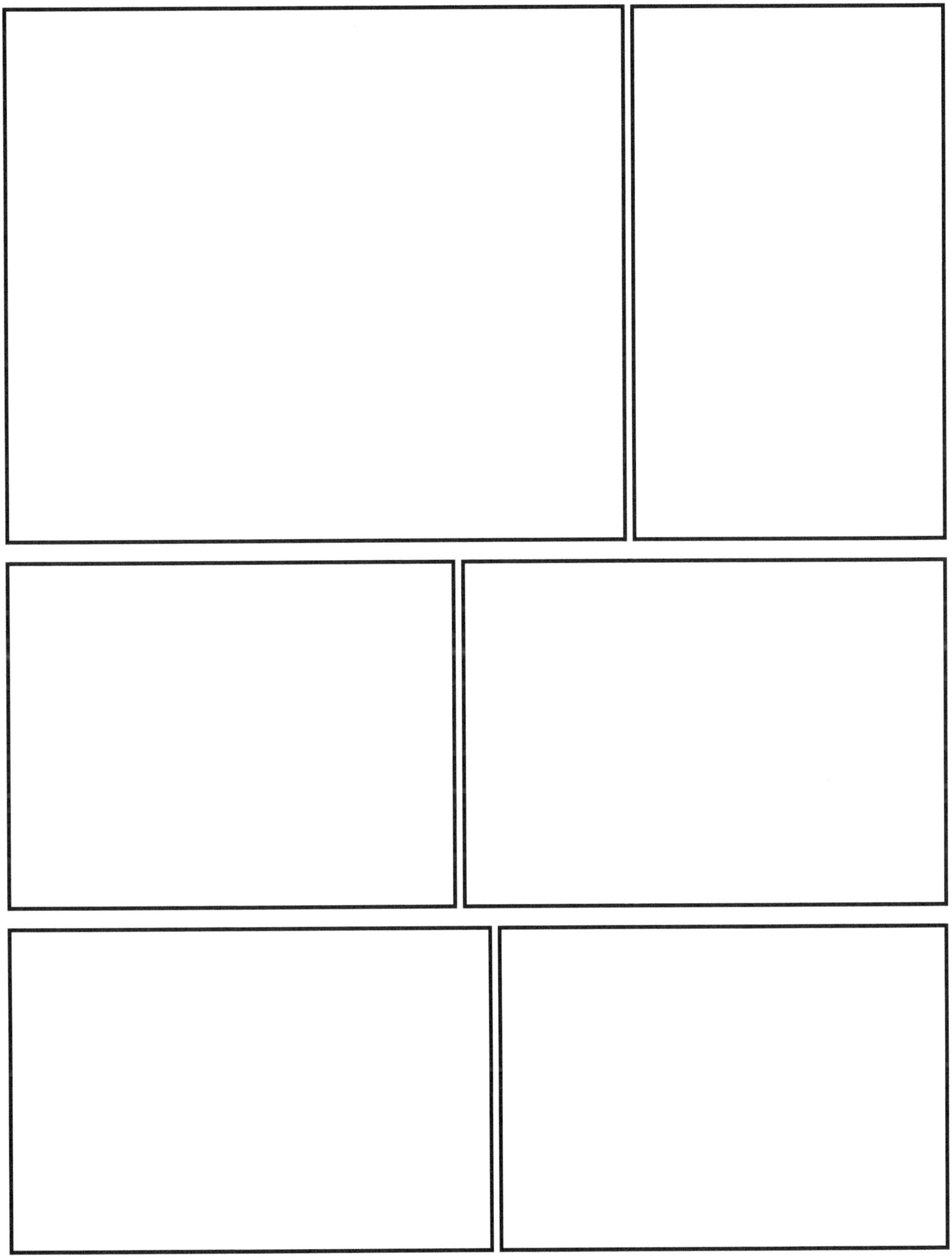

Now that your comics are done, why don't you tell your readers a little something about yourself?

And don't forget to add your portrait. In manga style, of course!

ABOUT THE AUTHOR/ILLUSTRATOR

YANCEY LABAT got his start at Marvel Comics before moving to illustrate children's books for many publishers, including Scholastic, Houghton Mifflin Harcourt, and Chronicle Books. He is the Ringo Award–winning illustrator of the best-selling DC Super Hero Girls original graphic novels, and a three-time recipient of the Diamond Comic Distributors Gem Awards for Best All-Ages Original/Reprint Graphic Novels. He lives with his wife and their two girls in San Carlos, California.

CPSIA information can be obtained
at www.ICGtesting.com
Printed in the USA
LVHW071056270720
661527LV00023BA/10